A MILITARY MISCELLANY

—A—
MILITARY
MISCELLANY

Important, Uncommon, and Sometimes
Forgotten Facts, Lists, and Stories from
America's Military History

THOMAS AYRES

BANTAM BOOKS

New York   London   Toronto   Sydney   Auckland

Published in the United States by Bantam Books, an imprint of Random House, a division of Penguin Random House LLC, New York.

BANTAM BOOKS and the HOUSE colophon are registered trademarks of Penguin Random House LLC.

Originally published in the United States by Bantam Books, an imprint of Random House, a division of Penguin Random House LLC, in 2006.

ISBN 9780385364911

Printed in the United States of America on acid-free paper

www.bantamdell.com

9 8 7 6 5 4 3 2 1

First Sterling Edition

Book design by Ellen Cipriano

To all the Americans
who have died for their country

A MILITARY MISCELLANY

INTRODUCTION

They have been called Yank, Grunt, Doughboy, Swabby, Flyboy, and GI Joe. From the Continental soldier whose rag-wrapped feet left bloody prints in the snow on his way to Trenton to the Marine dodging sniper fire in Baghdad, they always answer the bugle's call.

From 1775 to 2006, more than a million Americans have died in service to their country. Some lie beneath rows of white markers in manicured cemeteries, others in rural church graveyards just down the road from home. Some rest in unmarked mass graves in the fields where they fell. Yet, when duty calls, a new generation always rises out of the heartland to take their place.

The history of the United States is, in large measure, a story of military involvement. Our nation was born out of a revolution, and we rarely have been without a war since. It might come as a shock to some Americans to learn that the U.S. military has been called to invade other nations or territories some two hundred times. Our soldiers have been dispatched on great and noble missions, and at the whim of politicians with less than noble motives. They have been asked to save the world, and on occasion, to save Standard Oil and the United Fruit Company.

From the American Revolution to Iraq, most Americans are aware of our nation's big wars. But few realize that

United States Marines were fighting in Korea eighty years before the outbreak of the Korean War in 1950. It happened in 1871 when Koreans captured the American merchant schooner *General Sherman* and killed its entire crew. The U.S. Navy retaliated, destroying five Korean coastal forts. Two hundred forty-three Koreans were killed in the assaults. Four Americans died in the brief encounter. Do not look for this event in your American history book. You will not find it there. It is one of the scores of "little wars" that are a part of our forgotten military history.

Our involvement in foreign wars began when Thomas Jefferson dispatched warships to the coast of North Africa in 1801 to punish Muslim pirates terrorizing American sailors. Ironically, more than two centuries later, we find ourselves once more beyond the oceans at war in the Middle East. Between those conflicts, we have managed to fight ten major wars and, in 1861, when there was no outside enemy, we chose sides and fought each other.

What follows is historical miscellany—anecdotes, lists, little-known incidents, and interesting tidbits gleaned from the rich heritage of more than two centuries of almost constant American military involvement around the world.

Thomas Ayres

U.S. MILITARY PRODUCTION
IN WORLD WAR II

From mid-1940 until 1945, U.S. production of war materials overwhelmed the great Axis factories of Krupp (Germany), Fiat (Italy), and Mitsubishi (Japan). During the war, America produced:

Warplanes	296,429
Tanks	102,351
Artillery pieces	372,431
Trucks	2,455,964
Warships	87,620
Cargo ships	5,325
Aircraft bombs (in tons)	5,922,000
Small arms	20,086,061
Small-arms ammunition (rounds)	44 billion

≈ NOTABLE QUOTE

**"To American production, without which
this war would have been lost."**

*Joseph Stalin, offering a toast at a meeting of
Allied leaders in Tehran, Iran, 1943*

RATIONED AT HOME IN WORLD WAR II

Automobiles	Meats
Automobile tires	Cheese
Gasoline	Butter
Bicycles	Coffee
Bicycle tires	Cigarettes
Shoes	Lard
Sugar	Canned fish

* From February 1942 until the end of the war, no civilian automobiles or trucks were manufactured in the United States. When production stopped, there were 500,000 vehicles in stock. The government promptly took title to all of them, stored them in warehouses, and carefully doled them out to the military and to civilian applicants like country doctors, farmers, scientists, and individuals critical to defense production.

* Owning an automobile was not easy for a nonpriority citizen. A class "A" stamp on the windshield entitled the owner to only three gallons of gasoline a week. Many a vehicle sat idle because tires were unavailable and there were no parts for repairs.

* Some citizens began riding bicycles, until they also were rationed and replacement tires became unavailable. Walking was not a good option because civilians were limited to only two pairs of shoes a year. As a result, Americans witnessed a return of the horse and buggy in

some rural areas. Old bicycles built for two (popular at the turn of the century) were hauled out of barns and woodsheds, as were cars from another era. Baker Electric Cars made a brief comeback, and puffing Stanley Steamers, last manufactured in 1925, occasionally were seen.

"LUXURY" ITEMS UNAVAILABLE AT HOME IN WORLD WAR II

Hair curlers	Suspenders	Electric trains
Wigs	Rayon products	Cooking tongs
Kitchen utensils	Bronze caskets	Beer mugs
Lawn mowers	Electric toasters	Spittoons
Many paper products	Waffle irons	Cameras
Girdles	Eggbeaters	Birdcages
Nylon stockings	Tin soldiers	Cocktail shakers
Corn poppers	Leather	Sliced bread
Cast-iron skillets	Whiskey	Diapers

❧ NOTABLE QUOTE

And when I die, please bury me
'Neath a ton of sugar by a rubber tree;
Lay me to rest in an auto machine,
And water my grave with gasoline.

A popular homefront jingle in World War II

* From autumn 1942 to the summer of 1944, whiskey disappeared from store shelves. Enterprising distillers tried to bridge the drought with substitutes made from some unlikely products. Old Spud, distilled from waste potatoes, required a palate adjustment.
* While GIs lit up Camels and Lucky Strikes, civilian smokers puffed on strange-tasting new brands with names like Fleetwood. Many questioned whether these new cigarettes contained tobacco at all.
* Sliced bread became a delicacy of the past when the government removed slicing machinery from bakeries for the metal content. Bread came in whole loaves.
* Home-front fashion took a beating. Ladies' "stockings" came in a bottle and had to be painted on legs. Seams were drawn down the backs of legs with eyebrow pencils. Men's pants came minus cuffs and coats without lapels.
* Diapers were scarce. Moms coped by using scrap materials. Remarkably, a generation of U.S. babies survived.

WHEN THE U.S. ARMY INVADED RUSSIA

Unknown to most Americans and little noted by historians is the fact that 11,000 U.S. troops invaded Russia in 1918 and some remain buried there. Even as the U.S. entered World War I, civil war raged in Russia as the Bolsheviks

---

❄NOTABLE QUOTE

"There is many a boy here today who looks on war as all glory, but, boys, it is all hell."

General William T. Sherman, addressing cadets following the Civil War

tightened their grip on the country after overthrowing Czar Nicholas.

Anxious to assist remnants of the czar's White Army opposing the communist takeover, on August 15, 1918, President Woodrow Wilson broke diplomatic ties with the Bolshevik government. Within three weeks, 7,000 U.S. Marines had landed at the port city of Vladivostok on the coast of Siberia. Another 4,000 troops were dispatched to the far north of Russia to join British soldiers already fighting there. In Siberia, Marines fought beside their Japanese allies in support of the White Army.

In the north, the fighting was especially intense and American troops sustained several hundred casualties. The Marines in Siberia took lesser, but still significant, casualties.

In 1920, well after the end of World War I, and with the White Army defeated, Wilson quietly withdrew American troops. Although the venture was quickly forgotten in the United States, it was remembered in the Soviet Union. It set the stage for a cold war that would continue for most of the twentieth century.

🎯 IT'S A FACT

---

* Japan and Russia had been fighting over the sovereignty of several Pacific islands and Manchuria long before World War I. Japan also had ambitions to control part of Siberia. Technically, Japan and Russia are still at war, since both refused to sign a peace treaty at the conclusion of World War II.
* Casualty figures from America's involvement in Russia are included in World War I statistics and still cloaked in secrecy.

STONEWALL JACKSON'S
10 ECCENTRICITIES

1. He would bathe only in cold water, even in winter.
2. Refused to read by artificial light.
3. Would not let his back touch the back of a chair.
4. He thought his spine was out of alignment, causing his internal organs to be out of balance.
5. Believed one leg was shorter than the other.
6. Believed he did not sweat on one side of his body.
7. He would sit in silence and stare at a wall for an hour or more each evening.
8. Consumed large quantities of water at one time to cleanse his body.
9. He liked to suck on lemons.
10. Believed that holding his arm aloft helped keep his internal organs in balance and his blood circulating properly.

GENERAL PATTON'S 7 PAST LIVES

General George Patton was a devout believer in reincarnation. He believed in past lives he was:

1. A prehistoric hunter–warrior who "battled for fresh mammoth and warred for pastures new."
2. A Greek Hoplite soldier who fought against the Persians of King Cyrus.
3. A soldier in the army of Alexander the Great at the siege of Tyre.

4. Hannibal, crossing the Alps to invade Rome.
5. A legionnaire in the Roman army under Julius Caesar in northern Gaul.
6. An English knight in the Hundred Years' War who fought at the battle of Crécy.
7. A marshal in Napoleon's army at a time when "one laughed at death and numbers, trusting in the emperor's star."

2 WOMEN WHO BECAME WORLD WAR II AIR ACES

1. Lieutenant Lily Litvak, Soviet fighter pilot, seven kills.
2. Lieutenant Katya Budanova, Soviet fighter pilot, six kills.

The early air war between Germany and the Soviet Union took a heavy toll on Russian planes and pilots due to the superiority of German aircraft. Women were pressed into service to fill the depleted ranks of Soviet pilots. Both Budanova and Litvak died in combat when their planes were shot down in 1943.

❧ NOTABLE QUOTE

"Little Frenchman, I am going to fight Banks here if he has a million men."

General Richard Taylor to General Camille de Polignac just before his 8,800 rebels routed a 30,000-man Union Army at Mansfield, Louisiana

IT'S A FACT

Even in the heat of battle, General Thomas Jonathan (Stonewall) Jackson might be seen sitting on his horse, sucking on a lemon and holding one arm above his head. Those who knew Jackson were more amused than concerned by his eccentric behavior. They knew he was a hopeless hypochondriac. As a teacher at Virginia Military Institute, there was nothing about him to suggest to his students that he would become a famous general. They called him "Tom Fool" and drew caricatures with emphasis on his huge feet. They mocked his nervous mannerisms and imitated his awkward gait as he made his way across the campus. Jackson's hypochondria was not all in his imagination. He suffered from poor eyesight, a recurring throat infection, earaches, and chronic stomach gastritis. Modern doctors believe he might have suffered from peptic ulcers or even cancer of the stomach. In 1858 he had his tonsils removed, but it did not relieve problems with his throat. Contrary to the myth, Jackson did not believe lemons had special medical qualities. In fact, he never had any particular fondness for them until his troops captured a large quantity of lemons from the Union Army. After that he sucked on them to relieve the soreness in his throat. While still a teacher, he set aside an hour each evening for thinking. His wife was forbidden to disturb him as he sat motionless and stared at a wall. Gen. Richard Taylor witnessed similar behavior in the field, noting in his memoirs: "He [Jackson] would visit my campfire, sit and stare straight ahead for a time, then depart without ever having said a word."

EVOLUTION OF THE SUBMARINE

The concept of an underwater device for military use dates back to the Greeks and Romans, both of whom attempted to build such a craft. Milestones in the development of the modern submarine include the following:

1620—Dutch inventor Cornelius Drebbel constructed an underwater craft of leather and wood. He demonstrated it in the Thames River, taking it to a depth of fifteen feet.

1727—King James I of England reportedly rode in an underwater craft. By this date, fourteen different types of submarines had been patented in England.

1776—The first attempt to sink a ship with a submarine occurred September 7, 1776, when a one-man craft christened the *Turtle,* piloted by a Continental soldier named Ezra Lee, tried to attach a keg of dynamite to the British warship HMS *Eagle* in Long Island Sound. The attempt failed. The *Turtle* was an egg-shaped wooden craft built by a Yale student named David Bushnell.

1800—Working for Napoleon Bonaparte, inventor Robert Fulton designed and built a submarine he christened the *Nautilus.* Fulton made several successful test runs. The French lost interest in the project, and Fulton tried to sell his craft to the English. When a deal could not be made, Fulton abandoned the project and left the *Nautilus* to rot away.

1814—Bushnell built his second submarine during the War of 1812, but hostilities ended before it could be tried.

1861—The Union Navy launched a submarine named the USS *Alligator.* Designed by Marvin Thomas of Philadelphia, it was forty-seven feet long and had a crew of sixteen, including two divers who were to climb out of the craft and attach explosives to the bottom of an enemy ship. The *Alligator* was lost at sea while being towed to join the Union blockade at Port Royal, South Carolina.

1862—In the early months of the Civil War, at least three submarines were constructed at shipyards in New Orleans. They were scuttled when it became apparent the city would fall into Union hands in the spring of 1862.

1864—On February 17, the Confederate submarine *H. L. Hunley* rammed a torpedo into the Union warship USS *Housatonic,* sinking it in the harbor at Charleston, South Carolina. It was the first time a submarine sank a ship. The *Hunley* and its eight-man crew went down with the *Housatonic.* Two other *Hunley*-type subs were constructed but did not see action.

1892—Simon Lake, a Bridgeport, Connecticut, inventor, came up with the design for a craft he called a "Torpedo Boat." His concept became the prototype for the modern submarine.

HOW THE U.S. NAVY TURNED DOWN
THE SUB THAT BECAME THE U-BOAT

In the 1890s, inventor Simon Lake tried to interest the U.S. Navy in his design for a Torpedo Boat. Navy brass called the concept impractical and rejected it. However, the Russian Navy expressed interest and, determined to see his design become reality, Lake went to Russia and supervised the construction of the first practical, modern submarine.

By means fair or foul, the Germans obtained Lake's design, refined it, and built the U-boat that would devastate Allied shipping in World War I. Lake returned to the United States and established the Lake Torpedo Boat

Company. He built more than one hundred submarines during World War I—fifty-five for the U.S. Navy and the others for European allies.

U.S. ARMY MILITARY UNITS

SQUAD: Ten infantry enlisted personnel under a staff sergeant.

PLATOON: Four squads under a lieutenant.

COMPANY: Headquarters and four or more platoons under a captain. (An artillery company is a battery; cavalry, a troop.)

BATTALION: Headquarters and four or more companies under a lieutenant colonel.

BRIGADE: Headquarters and three or more battalions under a colonel.

DIVISION: Headquarters and three brigades with artillery and combat support units under a major general.

CORPS: Two or more divisions under a lieutenant general.

FIELD ARMY: Headquarters and two or more corps under a general.

THE DIFFERENCE BETWEEN A RIFLE AND A GUN

This is my rifle,
This is my gun.
One is for fighting,
The other for fun.

World War II drill sergeants used the rhyme to teach recruits the difference between the two.

JAPANESE BOMBARDMENT BY
BALLOONS IN WORLD WAR II

A long-kept secret by the U.S. government was the fact that in the waning months of World War II the Japanese launched several thousand "balloon bombs" at the United States. Approximately 1,000 of them rode the Pacific jet stream and reached the West Coast of the United States. Of those, only a few fell on U.S. soil and only one exploded and caused casualties.

Although little was known about the jet stream in 1944, Japanese scientists concluded that balloons launched into rapidly moving air currents some five miles above the earth would carry 6,000 miles to the U.S. mainland.

Almost all of the balloon bombs that reached the West Coast were shot down or otherwise intercepted by the U.S. military. However, several did come down on American soil, including one near Bly, Oregon. Several children and a woman examining the device were killed or injured when it exploded.

⬛ IT'S A FACT

---

* William (Buffalo Bill) Cody was awarded the Medal of Honor.
* Arthur MacArthur won the medal in the Civil War and his son, Douglas MacArthur, in World War I.
* Nineteen individuals have won the medal twice, among them, Thomas Ward Custer, the brother of George Armstrong Custer.

STORY OF THE MEDAL OF HONOR

America's highest military award for bravery was conceived by Adjutant General Edward Townsend and signed into law December 21, 1861, by President Abraham Lincoln. Before World War I, 2,625 medals were handed out, most of them during the Civil War, when the award was given freely. Every man in the Maine 27th Infantry got one as an incentive to reenlist.

An army review board later removed the names of 911 medal recipients as undeserving of the award, including all 846 given to the Maine 27th. To date, the following number of medals have been awarded.

Before World War I	1,714
World War I	124
Peacetime	18
World War II	464
Korean War	131
Vietnam War	245
Somalia	2
Iraq War	1 to date

❧ NOTABLE QUOTE

"Yesterday we rode on the pinnacle of success—today absolute ruin seems to be our portion. The Confederacy totters to its destruction."

Confederate General Josiah Gorgas, writing in his diary following rebel defeats at Gettysburg and Vicksburg

THE ONLY WOMAN TO WIN
THE MEDAL OF HONOR

There were only a few women doctors in the United States when the Civil War began. One was Dr. Mary E. Walker of New York, who immediately applied to become a surgeon in the Union Army. Rejected, she became a battlefield nurse and surgical assistant assigned to the 52nd Ohio Infantry.

In 1864, when her unit moved on, she stayed behind to treat Union wounded. She was captured and spent four months in prison before being paroled. Upon rejoining the Union Army, she was commissioned a lieutenant and became a "contract surgeon." Awarded the Medal of Honor, she proudly wore it everywhere.

Following the war, Dr. Walker became a campaigner for women's rights. Eccentric in manner, she tried to establish a separate colony for women only. In 1916, when a review board rescinded 911 Civil War Medals of Honor as inappropriate, Dr. Walker's medal was among them. She paced before the Capitol Building with a picket sign to protest the decision, to no avail. In 1977, President Jimmy Carter restored Dr. Walker's medal, making her the only female recipient of the honor.

THE YOUNGEST RECIPIENT
OF THE MEDAL OF HONOR

In the Peninsula Campaign of 1862, during the Union Army's retreat from Richmond, Willie Johnston of the 3rd Vermont was the only drummer boy in the division to emerge from the battle with his drum. On the recommendation of the division commander, he was awarded the Medal of Honor, becoming the youngest recipient of the award. He was thirteen years old.

2 CADETS WHO WERE
KICKED OUT OF WEST POINT

1. Edgar Allan Poe (1831)
2. Timothy Leary (1942)

⬤ IT'S A FACT

* Poe was expelled for disobeying an order and "gross neglect of duty."
* Leary left under threat of expulsion and later enrolled at the University of Alabama.

NOTABLE WEST POINT GRADUATES
AND HOW THEY RANKED

Douglas MacArthur (1903)	1 in a class of 93
Robert E. Lee (1829)	2 in a class of 46
William T. Sherman (1840)	6 in a class of 42
Omar Bradley (1915)	44 in a class of 164
Dwight Eisenhower (1915)	61 in a class of 164
George Patton (1909)	46 in a class of 103
John J. Pershing (1886)	30 in a class of 77
Ulysses S. Grant (1843)	21 in a class of 39
Jefferson Davis (1828)	23 in a class of 33
George A. Custer (1861)	34 in a class of 34

⬤ IT'S A FACT

Custer was as undisciplined in the classroom as he was in battle. He was on the verge of suspension with excessive demerits all four of his years at West Point and was under detention when he graduated at the bottom of his class.

5 WRITERS AND A CARTOONIST WHO WERE AMBULANCE DRIVERS IN WORLD WAR I

Ernest Hemingway
John Dos Passos
Dashiell Hammett
W. Somerset Maugham
Sidney Howard
Walt Disney

ROBERT E. LEE'S 4-POINT STRATEGY IN POSITIONING AN ARMY FOR SUCCESS

1. The defensive position should not appear too strong or the opposing army will not attack it.
2. It should give cover to the troops both from view and fire from artillery and have a good field of fire.
3. It should afford facilities for a counterattack.
4. It should afford facilities for pursuit.

2 NOTORIOUS INDIVIDUALS WHO WENT AWOL

JOHN DILLINGER—On the run from police for auto theft, Dillinger eluded arrest by joining the Navy in 1923. He served on the USS *Utah* for a year, becoming a fireman third class, before jumping ship at Boston. He became infamous as a bank robber and the first "Public Enemy No. 1," on the FBI's most wanted list.

JACK (LEGS) DIAMOND—Diamond was drafted into the army in World War I. He went AWOL, was captured, and spent a year in prison. He later became a mob boss in New York City and was arrested five times for murder before being gunned down by rival gangsters.

19 TERMS THAT ORIGINATED IN THE VIETNAM WAR

Band-aid—A medic

Beans and dicks—C-rations, hot dogs and beans

Beans and motherfuckers—C-rations, lima beans and ham

Boom-boom—Sex

Charlie—The enemy

Cluster fuck—An operation that goes bad or that is disorganized

Crispy critters—Burn victims

Diddy-bop—To walk carelessly in a combat situation

FNG—Short for Fucking New Guy, or a replacement

Frag—An attempt to kill a friendly officer with a grenade

Hump—To march or hike carrying a rucksack, or to perform any arduous task

John Wayne—A can opener. Also used to describe someone who acts like a hero

Lay chilly—To freeze or stop all motion when on patrol

Rabbits—Black vernacular for white American soldiers

Ringknocker—Military academy graduates, the reference being to the graduation rings they wore

Tiger suit—Camouflage fatigue uniform

Turtles—New troop replacements, because it took so long for them to arrive

FINAL WORDS

"They couldn't hit an elephant at this distance."

*Union General John Sedgwick just before he was killed by
a sharpshooter at Spotsylvania Courthouse*

"Sir, I am reading my Bible. I expect to be killed in
a few minutes."

*Sergeant Benjamin Wall's reply when his lieutenant asked
what he was doing. A few moments later he was killed in
a charge at the Battle of Mansfield*

"All right, men, we can die but once. This is the
time and place. Let us charge."

*Union General William Lytle, just before he was killed at
the Battle of Chickamauga*

"If you are not going, just move out of the way and
I will go ahead!"

*Gunboat Commander Thomas M. Buchanan,
ignoring warnings of rebel sharpshooters; killed as
he stood on deck, at Bayou Tèche, Louisiana*

5 HEROES WHO BECAME MASS KILLERS

JACK SLADE—Served with distinction in the Mexican
War (1846). Later became one of the West's most notorious killers. Hanged by vigilantes in 1864.

TOM HORN—A U.S. Army scout, he helped track down Geronimo. Later became a hired killer. Ironically, he was hanged for a murder he did not commit.

ALBERT DeSALVO—Joined the U.S. Army at age seventeen, served in Korea, and rose to the rank of sergeant in the military police. In the 1960s, he murdered thirteen women and became infamous as the "Boston Strangler."

ELMER BURKE—An Army Ranger in World War II, he destroyed a machine-gun nest, among other heroics. Highly decorated, he returned to civilian life to become a hired assassin.

HOWARD UNRUH—Won medals for bravery as a tank machine gunner in World War II. In 1949, he calmly gunned down thirteen people in Philadelphia in twelve minutes.

NATIONALITIES OF UNION SOLDIERS

(Based on 345,844 recruits entering service after March 6, 1863)

United States	237,391
Germany	35,035
Ireland	32,473
Canada	15,507
England	11,479
France	2,630
Scotland	2,127
Other	9,202

3 WARHORSES RIDDEN BY ROBERT E. LEE

1. Ajax—Lee's first selection for a warhorse proved to be too large and awkward for the battlefield and was returned to the farm.
2. Brown Roan—Ridden by Lee early in the war, this horse was retired due to blindness.
3. Traveler—The horse that carried Lee through the war had the temperament and agility suitable to the battlefield. Traveler is buried on the campus of Washington and Lee University.

THE BATTLE OVER A HAIRCUT

When an enlistee enters today's military, one of his first introductions is to the base barber, who shears his locks to the scalp. But in the Continental Army during the American Revolution, soldiers traditionally wore their hair braided in the back and secured by a ribbon.

Called a "queue" (or pigtail), it was proudly worn by officers and enlisted men alike. That changed in 1801, when General James Wilkinson issued an order requiring all soldiers to cut their pigtails. The edict was unpopular, but the men complied—with one exception. Colonel Thomas Butler, Jr., a hero of the Revolution, refused to cut his queue. His protest set off a four-year, one-man rebellion that inspired Congressional debate and eventually involved the President.

Because of his heroics in the Revolution, Butler was a favorite of George Washington. He also was popular among the troops and with members of Congress. For two years, Wilkinson ignored Butler's refusal to obey his order. But in 1803, when a controversy developed between the two officers, an angry Wilkinson ordered Butler arrested. He was found guilty of disobeying a direct order and spent six months under arrest. Andrew Jackson went to Washington to plead his case with President Thomas Jefferson.

Under pressure from fellow officers and Congress, Wilkinson restored Butler's rank and, once more, ordered him to cut his pigtail. When Butler again refused, Wilkinson had him hauled before another court martial. Found guilty, Butler faced a year in the brig.

Before the issue could be resolved, Butler contracted yellow fever. Sensing the end was near, he came up with a final act of defiance. He instructed his friends to bore a hole in the bottom of his casket.

"Let my queue hang down through it so that the damned old rascal may see that, even when dead, I refuse to obey his order," he told them.

Colonel Butler went to his grave with his pigtail dangling defiantly beneath his coffin. He would have been disappointed to know that Wilkinson was not there to see it.

≈ NOTABLE QUOTE

"It is well war is so terrible—we should grow too fond of it."

General Robert E. Lee following the Battle of Fredericksburg

AFRICAN-AMERICANS IN THE CIVIL WAR

African-Americans, both slave and free, played a major role in the American Civil War. By the end of the conflict, 178,975 black soldiers had served in the Union Army and engaged in 449 battles or skirmishes. Almost 30,000 others served in the U.S. Navy. By the end of the war, African-Americans comprised about one quarter of the Navy's manpower. More than 60,000 black soldiers and sailors died in the war—35,000 from diseases. The number of African-Americans who served in the Confederate Army is unclear. Slaves of light skin often accompanied their masters, enlisted as whites, and blended into the ranks. Some free blacks joined the rebel cause. In his book *Blacks in America's Wars,* historian Robert Mullen estimates that 93,000 blacks served in or with the Confederate Army, many of them as teamsters and laborers. Following are some of the battles in which black Union soldiers played a role:

Island Mound, Missouri (10-29-62)

Port Hudson, Louisiana (5-27-63)

Milliken's Bend, Louisiana (6-7-63)

Fort Butler, Louisiana (6-28-63)

Honey Springs, Indian Territory (7-17-63)

Poison Springs, Arkansas (4-18-64)

Brice's Crossroads, Mississippi (6-10-64)

Battery Wagner, South Carolina (7-18-63)

New Market Heights, Virginia (9-29-64)

Fort Gilmer, Virginia (9-29-64)

Saltville, Virginia (10-2-64)

Honey Hill, South Carolina (11-30-64)

Fort Pillow, Tennessee   Overton Hill, Tennessee
   (4-12-64)   (12-16-64)
Jenkins' Ferry, Arkansas   Fort Blakely, Alabama
   (4-30-64)   (4-9-65)

THE MILITARY ORIGIN
OF COMMON WORDS AND PHRASES

BAZOOKA—The shoulder-fired rocket launcher was named after a crude musical instrument used by comedian Bob Burns in one of his skits.

BUNK—Following the American Revolution, General Felix Walker was elected to Congress by the voters of Buncombe County, North Carolina. The general fancied himself an orator, an evaluation not shared by fellow Congressmen. Walker addressed the assembly at every opportunity, often at length on subjects clearly beyond his scope of knowledge. Each time he took the floor, he would preface his remarks by saying, "I speak for Buncombe." Speaking for Buncombe soon became a catch phrase for meaningless chatter. Shortened to "bunk," the word became a part of the English language.

GUNG HO—In the nineteenth century, when Westerners began pouring into China, they were awestruck by the Great Wall and other large public projects. They were especially fascinated by the Chinese ability to coordinate the labor of a large work force. On a signal from an overseer, the workers would chant "gung ho!" to synchronize their effort. The chant became a slogan for the U.S. Marine Corps under Lieutenant Colonel E. Carlson prior to World War II and eventually became an English expression for one who attacks a project with enthusiasm.

HIP—Following the Civil War, African-American musicians in New Orleans used discarded military instruments to create a new kind of music that evolved into jazz. The players often marched in parades. To keep them in cadence, the band leader would call out, "step! step! step!" much like an army drillmaster. Over time the cadence became "hep! hep! hep!" By the 1920s jazz musicians were being called hep cats. From "hep" evolved "hip," to describe a musician who was "in the know."

THE IMMELMANN MANEUVER—In World War I, German fighter ace Max Immelmann purportedly invented a combat maneuver in which he pulled his plane into a loop that brought him down on the tail of his pursuer. The maneuver made him famous. However, it did not prevent him from being shot down and killed.

 IT'S A FACT

James A. Garfield could write Latin with one hand and Greek with the other—at the same time.

THE MILITARY ORIGIN
OF COMMON WORDS AND PHRASES

CRANK—In medieval times, a dead soldier lying in a contorted position was referred to as a "crank." With the coming of the Industrial Age, the term was applied to a crooked metal shaft used to start an engine. The early automobiles were started with hand cranks. Although the electric starter long ago replaced the hand crank, drivers still "crank" their cars each time they turn the ignition key.

JEEP—In the mid 1930s, Elzie Segar, creator of Popeye in the "Thimable Theater" comic strip, introduced the

American public to a character named Eugene the Jeep. Segar's comic creation was a strange-appearing animal with super strength. With the approach of World War II, soldiers were introduced to a strange vehicle with the letters GP stenciled on it. In military language, that stood for "general purpose." However, the GIs associated the rugged little vehicle with the comic character and the GP became known as the Jeep.

MILESTONE—To determine how far Caesar's legions had marched in a day, stones were placed at equal intervals along Roman roadways. The stones were located every one thousand steps, each step being five feet. Experienced pacers were employed to make the markers consistent. This distance was called a "mille," Latin for one thousand. The mille was the ancestor of the modern mile. Translated into English, milestone came to symbolize a noteworthy event in one's life.

A STIFF UPPER LIP—Queen Anne of England did not like beards. To please her, British officers ordered men in the ranks to shave. The soldiers grudgingly did so, except for some who left a defiant growth on their upper lips. Although officers allowed the men to keep their mustaches, the slightest movement of the hair beneath a soldier's nose during inspection would bring a stern reprimand for breach of discipline. Thus, Queen Anne's finest learned to keep a "stiff upper lip" during inspections.

◉ IT'S A FACT

The average height of Union soldiers was 5 feet, 6.5 inches; average chest size, 35 inches. By contrast, the average height of today's soldier is 5 feet 8 inches and average chest size is 38 inches.

GRANT AND SHERMAN IN CIVILIAN LIFE

It is ironic that the two best Union generals had similar difficulties adjusting to civilian life in the interim between the Mexican War and the Civil War.

ULYSSES S. GRANT—Upon leaving the Army in 1854, Grant became a farmer but failed at the endeavor. He was unsuccessful as a real estate salesman. He worked as a rent collector but could not make enough money to support his family. With the help of his brothers, he went into business for himself, but it failed. In 1861, when called to duty, he was working as a clerk in a store owned by his brothers.

WILLIAM T. SHERMAN—As a civilian between wars, Sherman failed at every vocation save one. He failed as a banker, real estate agent, architect, and lawyer before finding his niche as an educator. Hired by the State of Louisiana, he established a military school that later became Louisiana State University. When Louisiana seceded, Sherman resigned his position and joined the Union Army. Although he was at the school for one year, he was so attached to his cadets he became choked with emotion and could not finish his farewell speech.

◉ IT'S A FACT

Following the Civil War, Grant became President and Sherman turned down a shot at the office with the famous saying: "If nominated, I will not run. If elected, I will not serve." Grant's Presidency was tarnished by corruption. When Grant was virtually broke late in life, Mark Twain urged him to write his biography, which he completed shortly before his death. Earnings from the book allowed his wife to live out her life in relative comfort.

THE LAST FULL MEASURE

Official Casualties in Major U.S. Wars

CONFLICT	NO. SERVING	BATTLE DEATHS	OTHER DEATHS	WOUNDED	TOTAL
American Revolution	250,000	4,435	NA	6,188	10,623
War of 1812	286,730	2,260	NA	4,505	6,765
Mexican War	78,789	1,733	11,550	4,152	17,435
Civil War, Union	2,213,363	140,415	224,097	281,881	646,393
Civil War, Confederate	1,000,000 est.	74,524	59,297	NA	133,821
Spanish–American War	307,420	385	2,061	1,662	4,108
World War I	4,743,826	53,513	63,195	204,002	320,710
World War II	16,353,659	292,131	115,185	671,846	1,079,162
Korean War	5,764,143	33,667	3,249	103,284	140,200
Vietnam War	8,752,000	47,393	10,800	153,363	211,556
Persian Gulf War	467,939	148	151	467	766
Afghan and Iraq	Ongoing	—	—	—	—

These are official U.S. government totals. Most historians agree that Confederate totals are grossly understated. An estimated 31,000 Confederates who died in Northern prisons are not included in the totals.

THE MOVIE STAR WHO WAS A SPY

During World War II, she provided U.S. and British agents with the names of Nazi sympathizers in her country. Because of her ability to travel without suspicion, she also carried coded messages for Allied intelligence. The spy was Swedish movie star Greta Garbo.

ARMAMENT OF THE MARINES
ON GUADALCANAL

In 1942 the best military equipment and supplies were going to the Atlantic Theater. This was the armament and equipment the 1st Marine Division carried ashore in the invasion of Guadalcanal:

1. 1,903 bolt-action, single shot Springfield rifles
2. Leggings from World War I
3. Cartridge belts from World War I
4. Browning machine guns from World War I
5. Mortars from World War I
6. Ammunition that had been in storage since World War I

* The invasion of Guadalcanal was the first attempt by the U.S. to retake an island in the Pacific. Eleven thousand Marines held a small strip of beach and a landing strip against massive Japanese assaults for two months before reinforcements arrived. The Japanese poured 50,000 men and tons of armament onto the island but could not dislodge the Marines.
* Other than the Japanese, the Marines' worst enemy on Guadalcanal was malaria. Quinine was unavailable. On any given day, 2,000 troops could be on sick call.
* The battle for Guadalcanal lasted six months, until the Japanese withdrew in February 1943. Casualties for Marine and Army personnel were 1,490 dead and 4,804 wounded. More than 25,000 Japanese were killed—many of them in banzai charges.
* In the air and naval battles that raged over and around Guadalcanal, the Japanese lost an estimated 600 planes. Both sides had twenty-four ships sunk, but the tonnage lost by the Japanese was much greater.

THE MILITARY ORIGIN
OF COMMON WORDS AND PHRASES

BIG SHOT—During the Civil War, inventor John Dahlgren developed a huge cannon. Called the Dahlgren gun, it had an eleven-inch bore. The Dahlgren made all other artillery pieces look small. Upon seeing it for the first time, Union soldiers were awestruck. They referred to the officer who commanded the gun crew as the "big shot." After the war, the words "big shot" came to symbolize a person of great importance.

BIKINI—In 1946 scientists exploded a test atom bomb on Bikini Atoll in the Marshall Islands. Several months later, skimpy, two-piece bathing suits appeared in store windows for the first time. Since the atom bomb was still big news, fashion experts called the swimsuits "bikinis" after the atoll where the explosion took place.

GREAT SCOTT!—At the outbreak of the Civil War, General Winfield Scott was the nation's highest-ranking officer. He was seventy-five years old and far too large to mount a horse, but his mind was still sharp. He drew up the Anaconda Plan, which the Union Army employed to squeeze the Confederacy into submission. Scott was a hero in the War of 1812 and the Mexican War, where he commanded the 1845 campaign that captured Mexico City. Vain and condescending to subordinate officers and men in the ranks, he was not well liked. The men referred to him derisively as "Great Scott!" In the Gay Nineties, almost thirty years after his death, "Great Scott!" inexplicably became a widely used substitute for swearing and is still used today to express surprise or awe.

HOOKER—The popular story is that this common word for prostitute comes from Union General Joe Hooker's declaration that association with ladies of the evening helped boost the morale of his troops. Supposedly, the general let prostitution flourish when he was military commander at Washington, D.C., during the Civil War. Actually, Hooker's stay in the nation's capital was brief and he never commanded the troops there. A more likely source for the name comes from New York City's notorious Corlears Hook neighborhood, where brothels lined the streets. Sailors from the nearby waterfront called the girls who worked there hookers.

TAILSPIN—Early in World War I, if a plane went into a downward spiral the pilot knew he was doomed. Engineers trying to solve the problem called it "autorotation." Pilots called it a "tailspin." Until 1916, no pilot had been able to pull out of a tailspin without crashing. When British pilot Eddie Stinson's plane began spiraling earthward, he figured if he was going to die he wanted to do it quickly. He gunned his craft and, to his amazement, the plane righted itself. Stinson's action solved a problem that had eluded aviation engineers. After the war, barnstorming pilots routinely thrilled air-show crowds by pulling out of tailspins using the lifesaving maneuver accidentally discovered by Stinson.

❧ NOTABLE QUOTE

"Give me Confederate infantry and Yankee artillery and I'll whip the world."

Confederate General D. H. Hill

THE "HELLFIGHTERS" OF WORLD WAR I

In France there stands a monument honoring the most decorated American military unit in World War I—the 369th Infantry. The men of the 369th were so ferocious in battle, the Germans called them the "fighters from hell." Ironically, the men of this storied unit did not fight beside their fellow Americans. Because they were black, they were assigned to the French Army and performed their heroics under the flag of France.

The 369th was formed as a National Guard unit in New York in 1913. They drilled on the streets of Harlem and met in an abandoned dance hall. When the United States entered World War I in 1917, they were among the first American troops sent to Europe. They performed labor duties until assigned to the French. Among their accomplishments:

★ They served in combat 191 consecutive days, longer than any other American regiment.
★ They were the first Allied regiment to reach the Rhine River.
★ They never lost a man to capture and never lost a foot of ground.
★ The regiment was cited eleven times for bravery.
★ By the end of the war, 171 officers and men of the 369th were awarded the Croix de Guerre by the French.

≫ NOTABLE QUOTE

"It was all my fault, all my fault!"

Lee to Pickett's men as they fell back from Cemetery Ridge

THE FIRST AFRICAN-AMERICAN GENERAL

Between the world wars, the "Harlem Hellfighters," as they became known, produced the first African-American general in the U.S. Army—Benjamin O. Davis. In World War II the unit fought in the Pacific Theater and was decorated for repulsing Japanese attacks on Okinawa. The war in Korea marked the last time they fought as an all-black regiment.

THE MOST DECORATED "HELLFIGHTER"

Henry Johnson was a railroad porter when he joined the National Guard unit that became the 369th Infantry. On May 14, 1918, he was on guard duty when the Germans attempted a surprise attack. The sentry with him was seriously wounded in the first exchange of fire, leaving Johnson to beat back the attack alone. Although wounded himself, Johnson killed four German soldiers and left thirty-two wounded on the field. He was awarded the Croix de Guerre with star and palm—France's highest military honor.

HOW 3 OFFICERS DEALT WITH INSUBORDINATION

GENERAL ISRAEL PUTNAM—Following the battle of Bunker Hill, Colonial soldiers were building breastworks under the watchful eye of Putnam. Riding down the line, he spotted a large rock and asked a soldier to place it on the wall. "Sir, I am a corporal!" the soldier protested. "I ask your pardon," Putnam replied. The general dismounted, picked up the rock, and placed it on the wall, to the delight of the men and embarrassment of the corporal.

GENERAL NATHAN BEDFORD FORREST—As his army crossed a rain-swollen stream, one of Forrest's supply wagons overturned. Fearing the mules might drown, he ordered a private to go into the water and cut the team loose. The soldier took one look at the swift-running current and refused. Forrest calmly dismounted, plunged into the stream, freed the mules, and led them to the bank. He then grabbed the private by the shirt collar and seat of his pants and hurled him into the stream.

LIEUTENANT JEFFERSON DAVIS—Assigned to duty at Fort Crawford—a remote outpost on the Mississippi River in southwestern Wisconsin—in 1831, young Jeff Davis, a lieutenant not long out of West Point, had difficulty earning the respect of the grizzled veterans stationed there. When a private refused to obey an order, Davis lit into him with his fists, instead of putting him on report. After beating the soldier into submission, Davis informed him that he would not report the incident since it was a fair fight. Davis had no more problems with insubordination.

THE PEACE PRESIDENT

Woodrow Wilson was known as the "Peace President" because of his attempts to establish a League of Nations following World War I. His record:

1. He sent troops to invade Mexico ten times during his administration.
2. Dispatched Marines to Haiti in 1915, killing some 3,000 Haitians.
3. Sent U.S. troops to occupy the Dominican Republic in 1916.
4. Sent troops to invade Cuba in 1917.
5. Dispatched U.S. soldiers to occupy Panama in 1918.
6. Sent soldiers to Nicaragua in 1918 to assure election of his hand-picked presidential candidate, then forced him to sign a treaty beneficial to U.S. business interests.
7. Sent an army to Europe to fight in World War I and "make the world safe for democracy."
8. In 1918, he dispatched troops to Russia to assist the White Army in its struggle against the communists.
9. In 1919 sent U.S. warships to blockade Russian ports.

3 DUELS THAT DID NOT TAKE PLACE

GEORGE WASHINGTON AND WILLIAM PAYNE—In 1754, Colonel Washington got into a heated argument with Payne over candidates for the Virginia Assembly. Payne responded to a personal insult by striking Washington with a stick. Several soldiers grabbed Payne, but Washington ordered his release. Everyone expected a challenge to a duel when Washington sent Payne a note requesting a meeting at the local tavern. When Payne arrived, he found Washington sitting at a table with wineglasses instead of pistols. To Payne's surprise, Washington apologized for the insult. "I was wrong," the future President said. "You have already had some satisfaction, and if you deem that sufficient, here is my hand." The two became friends and, from that day, Payne was an ardent supporter of Washington.

ANDREW JACKSON AND WAIGHTSTILL AVERY— Jackson and Avery were opposing lawyers in a 1788 trial when a heated exchange resulted in Jackson being accused of taking illegal fees. Jackson was furious. He ripped a page from a law book and scrawled a message demanding satisfaction. Aware of Jackson's reputation as a duelist, Avery's friends pleaded with him to call off the affair. Jackson refused and the two met on the field of honor. The peacemakers on both sides finally were successful in getting Jackson to call off the duel. Following an apology by Avery, the two fired their pistols in the air, ending the affair.

ABRAHAM LINCOLN AND AN UNKNOWN SOLDIER— When Lincoln was in the Illinois militia in the Black Hawk War, he got into an argument with a fellow militiaman. Unable to talk his way out of a challenge to a duel, young Lincoln reluctantly accepted. He sent word to his adversary that he was prepared to meet him. His choice of weapons was broadswords. Lincoln was an imposing physical specimen, standing six feet four and weighing over two hundred pounds. The prospect of facing such an opponent wielding a broadsword had a sobering effect on his much smaller challenger. Lincoln never heard back from him.

BARON VON WHO?

The two men perhaps most responsible for the Colonial Army's victory in the American Revolution might have been Pierre Augustin Caron de Beaumarchais and Baron Friedrich von Steuben. So what about George Washington and the Marquis de Lafayette? They were instrumental. The contributions of de Beaumarchais and von Steuben were vital to the outcome.

De Beaumarchais was a poet, playwright, Paris gadfly, and sometimes diplomat, who talked the King of France into providing gold, guns, ammunition, warships, and, finally, the French Army and Navy to support the American rebellion.

Von Steuben was the stern Prussian officer hired to whip Washington's undisciplined Colonials into shape and from whom the Colonial commander received a liberal education in military tactics. Although often ignored by historians, it is interesting to note that Washington's success on the battlefield improved considerably when von Steuben was present. That included the climactic Battle of Yorktown in 1781, where von Steuben was involved in planning the strategy that trapped the British Army against the ocean, ending the war.

"A BETTER JUDGE OF MEN THAN I"

While stationed at Fort Crawford, Wisconsin, in 1832, Lieutenant Jeff Davis became smitten with Sarah Taylor, the beautiful, eighteen-year-old daughter of Colonel Zachary Taylor, the post commander. Another daughter,

Anne, recently had married an army surgeon without Taylor's consent, prompting him to place his two remaining daughters "off limits" to post personnel.

When Taylor learned that Davis was seeing Sarah behind his back, the colonel announced his intention to shoot his young aide. Peggy Taylor managed to calm her husband before he could carry out the threat. Upon learning that Taylor had threatened to shoot him, Davis announced that he was going to challenge Taylor to a duel. Fellow officers restrained him until he calmed down.

Taylor transferred Davis to a post in St. Louis, well away from Sarah. Two years later, Davis left the army and he and Sarah were married in Louisville, Kentucky, where she was staying with relatives. Taylor did not attend. Tragically, Sarah contracted yellow fever and died just three months after the ceremony.

The estrangement between Davis and Taylor lasted for twelve years. In the Mexican War, Davis was in command of a Mississippi regiment in Taylor's 6,500-man army when the Americans came up against 15,000 men under Santa Anna at Buena Vista. Davis's troops turned back a massive cavalry attack on Taylor's left flank, assuring a U.S. victory. Afterward, Taylor thanked him and admitted, "My daughter was a better judge of men than I."

❧ NOTABLE QUOTE

"That old man had my division slaughtered at Gettysburg!"

A still-bitter George Pickett on Lee years after the ill-fated charge at Cemetery Ridge

HOW "FAT HENRY" BECAME A HERO

Following the Battle of Bunker Hill, Washington's Continental Army held the heights outside Boston, placing the British Army under siege. From out of the ranks, a young man came to Washington with a plan to fortify the position. The commander was so impressed he placed the soldier in charge of fortifications.

Next he told Washington that, without artillery, the British still might overrun the position. He reminded Washington that the abandoned fort at Ticonderoga in upstate New York had plenty of cannons just sitting there. He volunteered to lead an expedition to bring them to Boston.

Washington was doubtful that the guns could be moved in the dead of winter, much less all the way to Boston. His aides also were skeptical that an overweight city boy could brave the rugged wilderness and accomplish the task. With nothing to lose, Washington approved the expedition. What Washington did not realize was that this was no ordinary city boy.

Everyone called him "Fat Henry." He weighed almost 300 pounds and was something of a klutz. He even had two fingers missing from his left hand, the result of a hunting accident. He was a bookworm and, in fact, owned a bookstore. Well read on many subjects, his favorite topic was military history. He had studied all of the great battles of Europe and knew the most minute details about them.

Henry and several volunteers reached the fort in early December 1775. They strapped forty-three cannons and sixteen mortars on hurriedly built barges to float them down Lake George. They had barely departed when a blizzard descended on them. They abandoned the lake, built sleds, and purchased horses and oxen to tug the cannons over the snow.

Through dense wilderness, across frozen streams, and over the rugged Berkshire Mountains they moved southward, sometimes covering no more than a few hundred yards a day. Two more blizzards came, dropping temperatures below zero. Still they trudged on, defying the elements. Finally, two months after they set out on their journey, the party limped into Framingham, Massachusetts.

In the dead of one of the worst New England winters ever, Henry and his men delivered fifty-five artillery pieces weighing 119,000 pounds. Once the cannons were placed on the hills overlooking Boston, the British abandoned the city and sailed for Canada.

Fat Henry's real name was Henry Knox. He was twenty-four at Bunker Hill. By the time he was twenty-five he would be a brigadier general and Washington's artillery officer. He became the nation's first secretary of war, and Fort Knox would be named in his honor. He retired from public life at age forty-three. Of all his accomplishments, the least known might be his most important. During the war he started an artillery school that later became the U.S. Military Academy at West Point.

❦ NOTABLE QUOTE

> You're in the army now,
> You're in the army now,
> You'll never get rich,
> You son of a bitch,
> You're in the army now.
>
> *A favorite marching cadence of drill instructors*
> *welcoming recruits to the army*

WORLD WAR II AIR ACES BY COUNTRY

American aces from each branch of the U.S. military are included in the listing.

MAJOR ERICH HARTMANN, German Luftwaffe, 352 kills
CHIEF WARRANT OFFICER HIROYOSHI NISHIZAWA, Japan, 104 kills
CAPTAIN HANS H. WIND, Finland, 75 kills
MAJOR IVAN KOZHEDUB, Soviet Union, 62 kills
MAJOR RICHARD BONG, United States Air Force, 40 kills
WING COMMANDER J. E. JOHNSON, Great Britain, 38 kills
CAPTAIN DAVID McCAMPBELL, United States Navy, 34 kills
CAPTAIN PIERRE CLOSTERMANN, France, 33 kills
LIEUTENANT COLONEL GREGORY BOYINGTON, United States Marines, 28 kills

* Hartmann's total kills included 342 Soviet aircraft, seven U.S., and three British. He was twenty years old when he joined the Luftwaffe in 1941. He flew 1,425 missions and engaged in more than 800 dogfights. In one day in 1944, he shot down eleven Soviet planes. Hartmann crash-landed or parachuted to safety sixteen times. After the war Hartmann visited the United States several times and counted some high-ranking U.S. officers among his friends.

* Johnson's status as Great Britain's leading air ace has been challenged by historians. Squadron leader M. T. Pattle is believed to have shot down more than forty

enemy aircraft. However, some of his records were lost and not all of his kills can be confirmed.

* Boyington was commander of the famous Black Sheep Squadron in the Pacific Theater. Included in his total of twenty-eight kills are six Japanese planes shot down when he was with the Flying Tigers in China.

THE PRICE OF SOUTHERN SECESSION

1. One of every nineteen Southerners in the eleven seceding states perished during the Civil War. Equated to today's population in those same states, the death toll would be 4.6 million.
2. Including those who were killed and those who fled to other locales, the population of the South was reduced by 500,000 during the war.
3. One of every four white men of military age in the South died in the war.
4. Of the farms and plantations in the South in 1861, more than 400,000 were destroyed, abandoned, bankrupt, or otherwise insolvent at the end of the war.
5. Sixty-six percent of the assessed wealth of the South in 1861 had vanished by 1865.
6. In Mississippi, in 1866, twenty percent of the state budget was set aside to purchase artificial limbs.

≫ NOTABLE QUOTE

"War I despise. But if brought to my door,
I will be home."

James A. Garfield, Civil War officer and U.S. President

SURVIVAL STORIES OF
2 FAMOUS INDIVIDUALS

47 DAYS AT SEA

When American soldiers liberated a prison camp in Japan in 1945, among the inhabitants was an airman, more dead than alive. He weighed only seventy-seven pounds.

His name was Louis Zamperini. A decade earlier, he was one of America's most renowned athletes. In 1936 Zamperini was still in high school when he earned a spot on the United States Olympic track team. Sportswriters were predicting that he would become the best distance runner ever. But a youthful prank at the Olympic Games in Berlin not only cost him a chance to compete, it almost cost his life. On a dare, he tried to steal Adolf Hitler's personal flag. German guards caught him and almost beat him to death.

Recovering from his injuries, Zamperini returned to the U.S., where he shattered collegiate records in the mile run and came close to eclipsing the world record. With the outbreak of World War II, he became a fighter pilot. Shot down over the Pacific, he drifted in a raft for forty-seven days before being picked up by a Japanese patrol boat.

Zamperini survived two and a half years of hard labor, brutal treatment, and near starvation in a succession of prison camps before being rescued. After the war, Zamperini became a missionary. He returned to Japan, sought out the prison guards who had brutalized him, and forgave them.

LOST IN THE PACIFIC

On November 14, 1942, the crew of a Navy Catalina flying boat spotted a life raft bobbing like a white speck on the

Pacific Ocean, some 600 miles from the island of Samoa. There was a cheer from the crew when a flyover revealed three survivors. The most intense search–rescue mission of World War II was over.

The saga had begun on October 21, when an Army bomber ran out of fuel and went down with a very important passenger on board. Searchers found part of the crew stranded on a small island, but four were missing, including the VIP. For three weeks, search planes combed the area before the raft was spotted.

During the survivors' twenty-three-day ordeal, one member of the bomber crew had died and was buried at sea. Among the three who were rescued was Captain Eddie Rickenbacker, World War I fighter ace and one of America's greatest heroes.

THE LARGEST AIRBORNE ASSAULT

Contrary to popular belief, the largest airborne assault by paratroopers and gliders in World War II did not take place on D-Day, June 6, 1944. It occurred three months later on September 17, when three Allied divisions, totaling 34,000 troops, landed by glider and parachute at Arnhem, the Netherlands. The operation required 2,800 planes and 1,600 gliders.

❧ NOTABLE QUOTE

"Send me more men—and fewer questions."

*General Stonewall Jackson in a report to the
Confederate War Department*

15 WORST NONCOMBAT
MILITARY MARITIME DISASTERS

1865—*Sultana:* A steamboat carrying Union soldiers, many of them recently released from Confederate prisons, blew up and sank in the Mississippi River near Memphis, Tennessee; 1,450 fatalities.

1898—The *Maine:* U.S. battleship blown apart by a massive explosion in Havana Harbor; 260 fatalities.

1924—USS *Mississippi:* Explosion in gun turret of battleship off the coast at San Pedro, California; 48 fatalities.

1939—The *Squalus:* U.S. submarine mysteriously sank off the coast of New Hampshire; 26 fatalities.

1942—*Truxtun:* U.S. destroyer collided with the cargo ship *Pollux* and ran aground off the coast of Newfoundland and sank; 204 fatalities.

1944—Three destroyers in the U.S. Third Fleet went down in a typhoon in the Philippine Sea; 790 fatalities.

1952—*Hobson* and *Wasp:* The U.S. destroyer *Hobson* collided with the aircraft carrier *Wasp* in the Atlantic; 178 fatalities.

1960—*Constellation:* Fire broke out aboard the aircraft carrier docked at the Brooklyn Navy Yard; 48 fatalities.

1963—*Thresher:* U.S. Navy atomic submarine disappeared in the North Atlantic; 129 fatalities.

1967—*Forrestal:* U.S. aircraft carrier caught fire off the coast of North Vietnam; 134 fatalities.

1968—*Scorpion:* Nuclear submarine lost in the Atlantic near the Azores. Not located until six months later; 99 fatalities. Some say that the *Scorpion* was torpedoed by a Russian sub.

1969—*Evans:* U.S. destroyer cut in half in collision with Australian aircraft carrier *Melbourne* in South China Sea; 74 fatalities.

1981—*Nimitz:* A Marine combat jet crashed-landed on the deck of the aircraft carrier; 14 fatalities.

1989—*Iowa:* Explosion occurs in gun turret of U.S. battleship; 47 fatalities.

THE 25 BEST WAR MOVIES

(As selected by the author in no particular order)

All Quiet on the Western Front

To Hell and Back

The Longest Day

The Red Badge of Courage

Gettysburg

The Birth of a Nation

Midway

Patton

Saving Private Ryan

Platoon

Tora! Tora! Tora!

Apocalypse Now

Black Hawk Down

The Blue and the Gray (TV series)

The Blue Max

Friendly Persuasion

Memphis Belle

The Bridge on the River Kwai

The Patriot

Glory

Shenandoah

The Deer Hunter

Gods and Generals

Paths of Glory

Sahara

WHAT IF IT HAD NOT RAINED…

On August 28, 1776…General George Washington might have lost his entire army, and the American Revolution. On August 27, following a terrible defeat in the Battle of Long Island, Washington's Continental Army was trapped on the western end of the island. The British might have annihilated the Colonials but decided to wait until the weather cleared. Following a storm at sea, a thick fog enveloped the island, providing cover for the Colonials to escape across the East River to Manhattan Island and eventually to the mainland. Washington had lost New York but saved his army to fight another day.

On October 16, 1781...Lord Cornwallis's British Army might have eluded capture and prolonged the American Revolution. Cornwallis's army was trapped at Yorktown by a combined force of 15,000 American and French troops at his front and a fleet of French warships at his back. Outnumbered two to one on shore and unable to evacuate by sea, the British general came up with a bold plan to save his army. He would send his troops across the York River on barges under cover of darkness and try to link up with the British Army at New York. As the evacuation began, a violent thunderstorm descended. The barges were swept five miles downstream, where French soldiers captured a number of Cornwallis's men. More important, they confiscated the barges, eliminating Cornwallis's last hope of saving his army. Three days later, he surrendered.

On July 4, 1863...General Robert E. Lee might have lost the Army of Northern Virginia. On July 3, after two days of bloody fighting at Gettysburg, an impatient General Lee sent 11,000 men under General George Pickett against the strength of the Union Army holding Cemetery Ridge. Union artillery and a heavy concentration of infantry firepower cut the Confederate ranks to pieces. As the survivors struggled back down the hill, Lee's greatest fear was that Union General George Meade might counterattack his badly wounded army. That night, under the cover of a rainstorm, Lee began evacuating his troops. By July 4, he had completed the withdrawal, denying Meade a chance to attack and destroy the rebel army. Meade's indecision prolonged the war for almost two more years, costing hundreds of thousands of additional Union and Confederate casualties.

THE STRENGTH OF U.S. ARMED FORCES
(1789–2004)

1789	718	1910	139,344
1801	7,108	1920	343,302
1810	11,564	1930	255,648
1820	15,113	1940	458,385
1830	11,942	1945	12,055,884
1840	21,616	1950	1,459,462
1850	20,824	1960	2,503,631
1860	27,958	1970	3,064,760
1865	1,000,516	1980	2,050,627
1870	50,632	1990	2,043,705
1880	37,894	2000	1,335,923
1890	38,666	2003	1,375,489
1900	125,923	2004	1,377,221

 IT'S A FACT

Women make up fifteen percent of the nation's modern military. Nurses and medical personnel are included in the totals listed here.

SO YOU THINK *YOU'RE* UNDERPAID

* The pay period for Union and Confederate soldiers traditionally was every two months.
* A Confederate private was paid $11 a month, compared to $13 for a Union private. Rebel noncoms and officers received less pay than their Union counterparts. The highest pay for a Confederate general was $301, compared to $758 in the Union Army.
* Monthly pay for black privates in the Union Army was $10. However, a $3 uniform fee was withheld, leaving the soldier with $7. Some black soldiers refused to take any pay, in protest of the inequity. The policy finally was changed near the end of the war, and black soldiers received the same as their white counterparts.
* In the final two years of the war, pay was sporadic on the Southern side and the currency they received virtually worthless. Even in the early stages of the war, rebel soldiers often went several months without pay. Many rebel soldiers were not paid at all in the final year of the war.

ABOUT THE WORLD WAR II MEMORIAL

* DEDICATED: Memorial Day Weekend, May 29, 2004, in Washington, D.C.
* LOCATION: On the National Mall between the Washington Monument and Lincoln Memorial.
* MATERIALS: Bronze and granite. The granite was mined from quarries in Georgia and South Carolina.
* COST: $175 million. Although some public funds were used, most came from private donations. Schoolchildren

across the nation raised money for the project. Among those making large contributions was movie actor Tom Hanks.

★ ARCHITECT: Frederich St. Florian won a national competition to design the memorial.

★ PLACEMENT: The significance of placing the memorial between the Washington Monument and Lincoln Memorial: Washington was the key figure in the defining moments of the eighteenth century (the American Revolution and birth of the nation), and Lincoln in the nineteenth century (the Civil War that preserved the nation). World War II is considered the defining moment of the twentieth century.

★ THE DESIGN: The entrance features twenty-four bronze panels depicting World War II scenes. Two large arches (forty-three feet tall) represent the Atlantic and Pacific Theaters of the war. Fifty-six granite pillars, each seventeen feet high, surround a plaza. Each pillar is inscribed with the name of a state or territory from the period. A Freedom Wall is decorated with 4,000 gold stars, commemorating the more than 400,000 Americans who died in World War II. During the war, a gold star was presented to the families of soldiers who were killed. Mothers of slain sons were called "Gold Star Mothers."

❧ NOTABLE QUOTE

"A crow could not fly over it without carrying his rations with him."

*General Philip Sheridan after his army marched
through the Shenandoah Valley*

⊙ IT'S A FACT

---

* The erratic behavior of Confederate generals Braxton
  Bragg, Joe Wheeler, and John Bell Hood has been attributed by some historians to their consumption of whiskey
  laced with opiates.
* Following the Civil War, tens of thousands of drug-
  addicted veterans, North and South, returned home.
  Federal and state governments responded to their needs
  by supplying them with free morphine. The morphine
  came in small blue bottles. Because the containers were
  attractive to children, generations of daughters and
  granddaughters of Civil War veterans grew up collecting
  and playing with the blue bottles.

WHAT'S WRONG WITH THIS PICTURE?

In the famous painting of *Washington Crossing the Delaware,*
the most common criticism is that the general would have
known better than to stand in the bow of a rowboat in a
gale-tossed river in a sleet storm. However, there are far
more inaccuracies in the picture than the general's obvious
disregard for safety.

1. The Stars and Stripes flag shown in the painting did
   not exist until almost a year after the crossing took
   place.
2. The boats used by Washington's troops were forty to
   sixty feet long, not at all like the small vessel depicted
   in the painting.

3. No soldier would point the muzzle of his weapon sky-ward when it was sleeting.
4. In the painting, Washington is not crossing the Delaware. He is crossing the Rhine River in Germany.
5. The Continental soldiers in the boat are not Americans. They are Germans.

The famous painting was rendered by Emanuel Leutze in 1851, seventy-five years after the event took place. Leutze grew up in Philadelphia but moved to Dusseldorf, Germany, where he became an art instructor. He painted the scene in his studio, using art students as models for Continental soldiers and the Rhine as a backdrop for the storm-tossed Delaware.

TWO UNUSUAL APPOINTMENTS

1. General George Washington's choice for director of the Department for Detecting and Defeating Conspiracies, a division of his Headquarters Secret Service, was none other than Aaron Burr.
2. When Thomas Jefferson became president in 1801, the U.S. Navy consisted of a few aging warships and no one wanted the job of Secretary of the Navy. After being turned down by several potential appointees, Jefferson advertised the position in newspapers. He received only one response, that being from Robert Smith of Maryland. Jefferson hired him, and Smith served as Secretary of the Navy for nine years. In that time, he built the navy into a force that demanded world respect.

MONTHLY MILITARY PAY THEN AND NOW

RANK	UNION ARMY (1865)	U.S. ARMY (2006)
Recruit (Pvt. E-1)	13	1,178
Private (E-2)	13	1,427
Pvt. First Class	13	1,501
Corporal	13	1,663
Sergeant	17	1,814
Staff Sgt.	20	1,980
Warrant Officer	—	2,361.30
2nd Lieutenant	105	2,416.20
1st Lieutenant	105	2,783.10
Captain	115	3,221.40
Major	169	3,663.90
Lt. Colonel	181	4,246.50
Colonel	212	5,094.00
Brig. General	315	6,872.70
Major General	457	8,271.00
Lt. General	758	11,689.50
General	758	13,365.00

* Monthly pay scale for current U.S. Army personnel effective through 2003. Scale represents minimum pay based on two years or less at listed rank and varies with years of service. Pay for lieutenant general and general based on twenty years of service. Brigadier general through major general are limited to $11,875 per month regardless of length of service.

DRUGS AND MEDICINES
IN THE CIVIL WAR

During the war, the North could import the latest drugs from Europe, including critical supplies of quinine. Not so in the blockaded South. The Confederacy was forced to establish medical laboratories to produce drugs for military use.

These labs turned out medicines concocted, for the most part, from indigenous plants, including ground leaves, tree bark, and roots. By the end of the war, Southerners were demonstrating unusual inventiveness by developing experimental plant species with medicinal qualities through grafting and cross-pollination. They managed to produce opium, but a substitute for quinine eluded them. Quinine was the most valuable of all the war's medicines because it was effective in treating malaria as well as other ailments.

The most common medicine of the war, by far, was alcohol in the form of medicinal whiskey and brandy. Powdered leaves from toxic plants, opium, silkweed roots, cayenne pepper, and other questionable "medicines" were mixed with whiskey to treat a wide range of illnesses.

◉ IT'S A FACT

Gertrude Janeway, the last living widow of Union veteran John Janeway, died in January, 2003 at age 93. Alberta Stewart Martin, the last widow of a Confederate veteran, died in May 2004. She married William Martin in February, 1934 when he was 81 and she was 21.

AN UNUSUAL TREATMENT IS DISCOVERED

The Union infirmary at Chattanooga housed both Union and Confederate wounded. Doctors from both sides attended the men. In a period when medicine availability became extremely low, the Union soldiers had their wounds treated by chloroform and lint—the lint being used to keep maggots out of the wounds.

There was no medicine for the rebels, and their wounds soon became infested with maggots. That is when Confederate doctors made a discovery. The wounds of the rebels were healing faster than those of Union patients.

The Southern doctors knew nothing about bacteria, but they did know the maggots were keeping the wounds clean and the rebel patients were recovering more quickly than their Union counterparts. Although the evidence was clear, the Northern doctors continued to treat their soldiers with the prescribed medicines.

THE EVER-THINNING RANKS

A controversy over the location and design of the World War II Memorial delayed its construction for several years. Congress finally ended the squabble by approving the memorial. The reason: World War II vets, then in their seventies and eighties, were dying at an alarming rate, and lawmakers wanted to afford those who remained a chance to see the memorial.

Of the 16,000,000 Americans who served in World War II, less than 6,000,000 are still alive. The vets are dying at a rate of 1,100 a day, or more than 380,000 a year. Regrettably, they soon will go the way of the nation's Civil War veterans, who died off at an alarming rate in the 1930s.

PERILS OF BEING TREATED FOR DIARRHEA IN THE CIVIL WAR

More soldiers died in the Civil War from diseases than bullets. In fact, more soldiers died from diarrhea than were killed in battle. Treatments for diarrhea in the 1860s depended on the whim of the doctor, and the cure often was worse than the condition. For example: A soldier complaining of a three-month case of diarrhea was admitted to a Philadelphia hospital. He was treated with doses of lead acetate, opium, aromatic sulfuric acid, tincture of opium, silver nitrate, belladonna, calomel, and ipecac. He died in two weeks.

THE GREATEST AMERICAN NAVAL BATTLE

The greatest naval engagement of modern times was the Battle of Leyte Gulf in the Philippines from October 22–27, 1944. Involved in the six-day sea–air struggle were 231 ships and 1,996 aircraft. Of the sixty-five Japanese ships engaged, thirty-three were sunk. The Allies lost only six ships out of a fleet of 166. However, the all-time greatest sea battle in terms of the number of ships and men involved took place in 480 B.C., when a Greek fleet of 310 ships defeated a Persian armada of more than 800 vessels with more than 30,000 men involved on both sides.

OFFICERS KILLED
BY THEIR OWN TROOPS

1. General Thomas "Stonewall" Jackson—At the Battle of Chancellorsville, on the night of May 2, 1863, Jackson was returning from a scout behind Union lines with several of his staff when they were mistaken for Yankee cavalry. North Carolina troops fired on them, mortally wounding Jackson. Doctors amputated his left arm, but he died eight days later of pneumonia. Informed of his death, Robert E. Lee said: "Jackson lost his left arm. I have lost my right."

2. General Albert S. Johnston—On April 6, 1862, at the Battle of Shiloh, Commanding General Johnston's rebel army appeared on the brink of victory when several of his regiments refused to advance. Johnston went to the front to rally the men. He was preparing to lead a charge when a bullet fired by one of his troops struck his leg. Thinking it was a minor wound, Johnston ignored it until he began reeling in the saddle and a staff officer had to keep him from falling. When Johnston's boot was removed, it was soaked with blood. Within minutes he bled to death. The charge stalled, allowing General Ulysses Grant's Union Army to narrowly escape a disastrous defeat.

3. General Thomas Williams—The Union commander at the Battle of Baton Rouge was attempting to rally his troops for a counterattack when he was struck in the chest by a bullet fired by one of his soldiers. Almost at the same instant, second-in-command General G. T. Roberts was killed, also possibly by friendly fire. Although the infantry was routed at Baton Rouge, fire

from gunboats stopped the Confederate advance, preserving a Union victory.

4. Colonel David Marcus—Marcus resigned his position at the Pentagon to enlist in the newly formed Israeli Army. On the night of June 10, 1948, during the Israeli War for Independence, he was shot and killed while urinating in a field. One of his own sentries mistook him for an Arab since he had a bedsheet wrapped around him.

5. Lieutenants Richard Harlan and Thomas Dellwo— Early in the morning of March 16, 1971, someone at the U.S. Army base in Bienhoa, Vietnam, cut a hole in the screen covering the offices' quarters and threw a fragmentation grenade inside. Harlan and Dellwo were killed. Private Billy Dean Smith was arrested and court-martialed for the crime but was found innocent. The perpetrator of the crime was never determined.

6. Maj. Gregory Stone and Capt. Chris Seifert—On March 23, 2003, in an attack prosecutors say was motivated by religious extremism, Sgt. Hasan Akbar threw grenades into military command center tents in Kuwait, killing Capt. Chris Seifert. Major Gregory Stone died several days later, and 14 others were wounded. Two years later, a military jury found Akbar guilty of premeditated and attempted murder. He is currently on death row awaiting appeal.

A PREDICTION THAT CAME TRUE

"If the Japanese attack us, it will be at Pearl Harbor."

—*General George S. Patton in a letter written in 1936*

MILITARY WEAPONS NAMED
FOR THEIR INVENTORS

COLT REVOLVER (1836)—Samuel Colt was sixteen when he ran away from home and went to sea. Aboard the ship, he carved a wooden replica of a pistol with a revolving chamber. In 1836, when he was only twenty-two years old, he built a revolver and got a patent. In 1855 he finally began mass-producing the weapon. The Colt revolver was the handgun of choice in the Civil War, and his "six-shooter" became the storied weapon that tamed the American West.

GATLING GUN (1862)—Dr. Richard J. Gatling was trained to save lives, not to build a rapid-fire weapon capable of destroying them. Although he studied medicine, he never practiced as a doctor. He was an inventor, specializing in producing agricultural equipment when the Civil War began. Gatling developed a crank-operated forerunner of the machine gun in 1862. He thought the weapon would create such horrific casualties it would end warfare. Union military experts were not impressed and rejected the weapon for almost two years. It finally was adopted after Gatling hired a civilian crew to demonstrate its effectiveness in a combat situation.

WINCHESTER RIFLE (1867)—Oliver F. Winchester was a successful manufacturer of shirts when he became interested in weapons. In 1857, he purchased the Volcanic Repeating Arms Company. An astute businessman, Winchester hired the best inventors and gun designers away from competitors and bought up patents. In 1867, he established the Winchester

Repeating Arms Company. His rifle became the favorite weapon of the American frontier. Winchester virtually monopolized the repeating–rifle market for the last half of the nineteenth century.

MAXIM MACHINE GUN (1883)—Sir Hiram Maxim was a remarkable inventor—a pioneer in the development of nineteenth-century automotive and aviation science. He even built a multiwing aircraft well before the Wright brothers and managed to briefly get it off the ground before it crashed. Born in the United States, he moved to England in 1881 at age forty-one. In 1883 he produced the first modern machine gun and built a factory to manufacture it. During his career, he was granted 122 patents in the United States and 149 in Great Britain. His formulas for aviation thrust and lift were used by early aircraft builders (including the Wright brothers) to produce the first practical airplanes. For his scientific contributions, he was knighted by Queen Victoria.

THOMPSON SUBMACHINE GUN (1920)—General John T. Thompson was a West Point graduate who served in the U.S. Army's Ordnance Department. Following World War I, in 1920, he invented the rapid-fire submachine gun, which proved to be a deadly close-range weapon. It was first used as a military weapon in 1926 when U.S. Marines invaded Nicaragua. In the 1930s the "Tommy gun" became the weapon of choice for both gangsters and the FBI. Variations of the gun were used by both sides during World War II.

GARAND M1 RIFLE (1930)—John C. Garand became interested in weapons while managing a shooting gallery. He later went to work for the federal government at the U.S. Armory in Springfield, Massachusetts, and perfected a semiautomatic rifle he had been working on for years. In 1936, the U.S. Army approved his rifle, and it became the standard infantry weapon for soldiers in World War II and Korea. Although millions of Garand M1's were produced, Garand never received royalties or other compensation, because he was a government employee when he developed the weapon.

A PASS TO RICHMOND

President Lincoln told the story of a man who petitioned him for a pass to visit Richmond, the Confederate capital. Lincoln told him he would gladly give him a pass but said it might not be any good. "I have given two hundred and fifty thousand passes to men to go to Richmond in the past two years and not one has gotten there."

LAST LIVING VETERANS

Is it possible that a Civil War veteran could live to witness the beginning of the space age or that a soldier in the Spanish-American War would survive to see the birth of the World Wide Web? It not only is possible, it happened.

AMERICAN REVOLUTION—Daniel F. Bakeman, died
    April 5, 1869 at age 109
WAR OF 1812—Hiram Cronk, died May 13, 1905 at age 105
MEXICAN WAR—Owen Thomas Edgar, died September
    3, 1929 at age 98

CIVIL WAR, UNION—Albert Woolson, died August 2, 1956 at age 109

CIVIL WAR, CONFEDERATE—John Salling, died March 16, 1958 at age 112

SPANISH-AMERICAN WAR—Nathan E. Cook, died September 10, 1992 at age 106

FOUR ERRONEOUS PREDICTIONS

1. "The South has too much common sense and good temper to break up the Union."—Presidential candidate Abraham Lincoln, 1860
2. "Believe me, Germany is unable to wage war."—David Lloyd George, British Prime Minister, 1934
3. "No matter what happens, the United States Navy is not going to be caught napping."—Frank Knox, U.S. Secretary of the Navy, three days before the attack on Pearl Harbor
4. "The United States will not be a threat to us for decades—not in 1945 but at the earliest in 1970 or 1980."—Adolf Hitler in 1940

◉ IT'S A FACT

Beginning in 1931, ten years before the attack on Pearl Harbor, every graduate of the Japanese Naval Academy had to answer the following hypothetical question as part of his final exam: "How would you carry out a surprise attack on Pearl Harbor?" The question was removed from the examination after December 7, 1941.

TO THE SHORES OF TRIPOLI:
AMERICA'S FIRST FOREIGN WAR

With the signing of the Paris Peace Treaty between Great Britain and the United States in 1783, the founding fathers began the daunting task of establishing a fledging republic in America. Even as they struggled to do so, an incident took place thousands of miles away that would test their resolve.

The Barbary pirates seized an American merchant ship off the coast of North Africa and took the crew captive. Some were sold into slavery, others were held for ransom. There was little the Congress could do about it, because George Washington was in the process of disbanding what was left of the Continental Army, there was no effective navy, and no money to finance one.

It was a bitter pill for a nation that had just emerged triumphant from a seven-year war, in which Americans fought the mighty British Empire to a standstill.

The Barbary pirates had prowled the Mediterranean and plundered European shipping for two centuries before America gained its independence. The pirates operated under the protection of four North African Islamic states—Tunisia, Algiers, Morocco, and Tripolitania. Those enclaves of extortion demanded tribute; otherwise, they would unleash their state-sponsored pirates to attack the ships of nonpaying nations.

Without a navy capable of contending with the pirates, the U.S. Congress had little choice but to pay tribute. However, payments were sporadic, and the pirates continued to attack American ships.

By the end of President George Washington's first term,

Algiers alone was holding eleven American vessels and 115 sailors for ransom. Unable to ignore the outrage of family members of the captive sailors, some of whom had been held for ten years, Congress paid Algeria $1 million to ransom 115 Americans and agreed to pay an annual tribute of $21,000. Meanwhile, the other three Islamic nations also demanded tribute.

When Thomas Jefferson became president in 1801, he sent warships to the Mediterranean to challenge the pirates. In 1805 a second fleet was dispatched. This time, U.S. Marines went ashore to capture the fortress at Derna east of Tripoli and free hostages. In 1815, following a series of battles with the pirates, the United States emerged victorious and forced the Barbary states to sign a treaty, finally allowing freedom of passage for American ships in the Mediterranean.

LEADING U.S. WORLD WAR I AIR ACES

PILOT	KILLS
Edward V. Rickenbacker	26
Frederick W. Gillette	20
Wilfred Beaver	19
Howard A. Kullberg	19
William C. Lambert	18
Frank Luke	18
August T. Iaccaci	17
Paul T. Iaccaci	17
Eugene S. Coler	17
Raoul Lufbery	16

⭐ IT'S A FACT

* There were ninety-nine European pilots with more kills than Rickenbacker. Top ace of the war was Germany's Manfred Freiherr von Richthofen, better known as the Red Baron, who shot down eighty Allied planes. The leading Allied ace was Rene Fonck, with 76 kills. Because of America's late entry into World War I, most U.S. pilots spent less than a year in combat. Some European fliers spent three years engaging in dogfights, accounting for their large number of kills.

* For many years Captain Roy Brown, a Canadian in the Royal Air Force, was credited with shooting down the legendary Red Baron. However, a study of autopsy reports and recently discovered written eyewitness accounts have proven that the bullet that killed the legendary ace came from ground fire, and not from Captain Brown's aircraft. The man who fired the fatal bullet was an Australian machine-gunner named Sergeant Cedric Popkin.

EYEWITNESS TO HISTORY

One man was present at three historic events in World War II:

1. The attack on Pearl Harbor.
2. The dropping of the A-bomb on Hiroshima.
3. The Japanese surrender ceremony aboard the USS *Missouri*.

He was Japanese Commander Mitsuo Fuchida, the man who led the attack on Pearl Harbor with the war cry "Tora!

Tora! Tora!" Fuchida was flying to Hiroshima when he saw the nuclear mushroom cloud rise over the city. And he was on the *Missouri* as part of the surrender ceremonies that ended the war in the Pacific.

After the war, Fuchida converted to Christianity and became an evangelist. He visited the United States many times before his death at age seventy-three.

COST OF THE GREAT DEPRESSION

When the first draftees were called up by the Selective Service in 1940, government officials were stunned to discover that forty percent could not pass the physical examination. National Physical Fitness Director John B. Kelly blamed widespread malnutrition and poor health care for children in the Great Depression. The most common causes for rejection, in order of prevalence, were:

1. Bad teeth
2. Poor eyesight
3. Heart disease
4. Poor circulation
5. Deformities of arms and legs
6. Mental disorders

◉ IT'S A FACT

---

* Many volunteers did not meet weight requirements for their height. Recruiters routinely told them to go home and eat bananas until they reached the required weight.
* John B. Kelly was the father of Grace Kelly, the film actress who became princess of Monaco.

TRIPOLI'S TRIBUTE DEMANDS

Following is a list of tributes demanded by Tripoli in 1797 in exchange for American merchant ships to operate freely in the Mediterranean:

* Gold and silver coins totaling $40,000
* $12,000 in Spanish currency
* Five rings—three with diamonds, one with a sapphire, and one with a watch
* 141 ells of cloth
* Four caftans of brocade

Without a navy to contend with the Barbary pirates, the United States met the demand.

DEATH RATES OF U.S. POWS
IN WORLD WAR II

The percentage of deaths of American prisoners of war held by enemy countries:

1. Germany   1 of 100 died in captivity
2. North Vietnam   15 of 100 died in captivity
3. Japan   39 of 100 died in captivity
4. North Korea   40 of 100 died in captivity

THE GHOST FLEET

On the night of July 26, 1942, a fleet of fifteen U.S. warships was operating south of the Aleutian Islands when their radars picked up images that convinced commanders a Japanese convoy was headed for Kiska Island to resupply enemy troops. The U.S. ships opened up and continued firing on the position of the radar images for a full thirty minutes. When scout ships were sent to check on the enemy fleet, not a single vessel was found. The mystery of the "ghost fleet" radar images was never resolved. Technicians speculated that it might have resulted from freakish weather conditions that caused radar impulses to reflect off Alaskan mountain peaks. If that was the case, there is a possibility that the U.S. fleet was firing at the reflected images of its own ships.

HOW TALL WERE THEY?

George Washington	6'2"	John J. Pershing	5'9"
Andrew Jackson	6'0"	Douglas MacArthur	6'0"
William H. Harrison	5'8"	George Patton	5'11"
Zachary Taylor	5'9"	Benedict Arnold	5'9"
Abraham Lincoln	6'4"	Robert E. Lee	5'8"
Ulysses S. Grant	5'8"	Stonewall Jackson	6'0"
Theodore Roosevelt	5'8"	George McClellan	5'7"
Lt. Harry S. Truman	5'8"	William T. Sherman	5'10"
Dwight D. Eisenhower	5'10"	Horatio Nelson	5'5"
John Kennedy	6'1"	Napoleon Bonaparte	5'6"
Jimmy Carter	5'10"	Hirohito	5'5"
George H. W. Bush	6'2"	George W. Bush	5'11"

 IT'S A FACT

Claims that Napoleon stood only 5 feet 3 inches are in error.

8 GENERAL AFFAIRS

Commanding generals who went beyond the call of duty to conquer—mistresses.

1. **SIR WILLIAM HOWE**—The commander of British forces in the American Revolution had an open affair with the wife of a subordinate officer. The affair inspired soldiers in the ranks to make up a song:

   > *"Sir William he, snug as a flea,*
   > *Lay all this time a' snoring;*
   > *Nor dreamed of harm as he lay warm,*
   > *In bed with Mrs. Loring."*

2. **GEN. JOHN BURGOYNE**—In 1777, Burgoyne brought an 8,000-man British army from Canada to invade upstate New York. He also brought his fun-loving mistress. One of his soldiers wrote that the general spent his nights "singing, drinking, gambling, and carousing with his mistress." He should have gotten more rest. After a series of battles at Saratoga, his entire army was cut off and captured.

3. **GEN. JUDSON KILPATRICK**—During the Civil War, this Union general not only was accompanied by his mistress, he had her outfitted in a matching uniform. He got in trouble when she started trying to boss the troops.

4. **GEN. EARL VAN DORN**—The Confederate commander of troops in Arkansas and Mississippi found time to have an affair with the wife of a doctor in his army. The spurned doc shot Van Dorn in the back and fled behind Union lines, where he was welcomed as a hero.

5. **GEN. GEORGE PATTON**—While stationed in Hawaii in the 1930s, Patton allegedly had an affair with his niece. He survived the scandal to become commander of the Third Army in World War II.

6. **GEN. DOUGLAS MacARTHUR**—Assigned to command in the Philippines, MacArthur was sailing to Manila when he became involved in a romance with a woman half his age. They lived together in a luxury apartment in Manila during his tour of duty there. MacArthur later paid her $15,000 to keep quiet about their relationship.

7. **GEN. DWIGHT D. EISENHOWER**—The commander of Allied Forces in World War II, Eisenhower had an affair with his attractive chauffeur, Kay Summersby.

8. **GEN. DAVID HALE**—In 1998, Hale was one of the nation's highest-ranking officers. Accused of having affairs with the wives of several subordinate officers, he was forced to resign from the U.S. Army.

AMERICA'S FIRST UNPOPULAR WAR

Resistance to the War in Vietnam inspired widespread demonstrations and pitched battles between police and riotous crowds. But it might not have been America's *most* unpopular conflict. The War of 1812 threatened to split the nation in two when representatives from the New England states met in convention at Hartford, Connecticut, to consider seceding from the United States.

There were no riotous demonstrations in the streets, but opposition to the War of 1812 was just as emotional and intense as that during the Vietnam conflict. It has been estimated that perhaps half of the U.S. population opposed it.

Only the tone of the demonstrations was different. One woman drew a crowd by cutting her hair in public. She delivered it to First Lady Dolley Madison's sister and expressed her desire that the locks be woven into a rope with which President James Madison could hang himself.

New England's political leaders called the conflict "Virginia's war" and "Madison's war" and refused to support it. Many Americans not only opposed the war but openly aided the British invaders.

As British troops advanced on Washington, D.C., Dolley Madison fled the city, seeking sanctuary at a house not far from the capital. The woman who lived there was antiwar and refused to help her. The First Lady ended up hiding out in a tavern.

General Andrew Jackson's decisive victory at the Battle of New Orleans helped unify the nation. As word of his victory spread, the battle achieved legendary status and inspired a renewal of nationalistic pride. Ironically, because of poor communications, the battle was fought after a peace treaty was signed and the war was over.

⬗ IT'S A FACT

---

* In twenty-one days, Jackson's small army marched 225 miles, fought in three major battles, four engagements, and numerous skirmishes. In doing so, he tied up 75,000 Union troops, including General McDowell's 20,000-man army, and delayed a federal attack on Richmond. Jackson's Valley Campaign tactics are still studied in military academies.
* A joke circulated that Jackson was using Union General Banks's supply train as his personal commissary. It earned Banks the nickname "Commissary Banks."

THE ONLY PRESIDENT WHO
PARTICIPATED IN A BATTLE

President James Madison is the nation's only commander in chief who, as President, actually went to the front to observe a battle. It happened in the War of 1812 when the British were advancing on Washington, D.C. Madison went to the front to inspect the troops. When the British attacked, he remained there, thinking he would be an inspiration to the men.

Regrettably, the U.S. defenders were under the command of General William Winder, a notorious incompetent who had previously been relieved of command after a disastrous defeat at the Battle of Stoney Creek in Canada. The disciplined British troops quickly routed Winder's disorganized forces, and Madison barely avoided capture by the rapidly advancing enemy. He fled to safety at Wiley's Tavern and hid out there with his wife while the British burned the nation's capital and departed.

DATELINE

PARIS, France (April 14, 1905)—A longtime mystery was solved when the body of American naval hero John Paul Jones was unearthed from an unmarked grave in a Paris cemetery.

◉ IT'S A FACT

At least fifteen Confederate and twenty-six Union generals died of various diseases during the Civil War.

CIVIL WAR GENERALS WHO BECAME PRESIDENT

1. Andrew Johnson (1865–1869)
2. Ulysses S. Grant (1869–1877)
3. Rutherford B. Hayes (1877–1881)
4. James Garfield (1881)
5. Benjamin Harrison (1889–1893)
6. William McKinley (1897–1901)

◉ IT'S A FACT

James Garfield and William McKinley survived the war, only to be assassinated in office.

CIVIL WAR GENERALS WHO RAN FOR PRESIDENT AND WERE DEFEATED

1. George McClellan (lost in 1864)
2. Winfield Hancock (lost in 1880)
3. John W. Phelps (lost in 1880)
4. James B. Weaver (lost in 1880 and 1892)
5. Neal Dow (lost in 1880)
6. Benjamin Butler (lost in 1884)
7. Clinton B. Fisk (lost in 1888)

◉ IT'S A FACT

In the wild election of 1880, Phelps ran as the candidate of the Anti-Masonic Party. Weaver was the selection of the Greenback Party, and Dow represented the Prohibition Party. Garfield, the Republican nominee, won the election. Weaver ran unsuccessfully for President a second time in 1892, as nominee of the People's Party.

6 FAMOUS CIVIL WAR HORSES
KILLED IN BATTLE

1. Beauregard—Ridden by Confederate General Wade Hampton; killed in 1863.
2. Beppo—Owned by Union General Judson Kilpatrick; killed in battle at Aldie, Virginia.
3. Billy—Owned by Union Lt. Frank Haskell; became famous for carrying the lieutenant to safety after being shot through the lungs.
4. Chancellor—Confederate General J.E.B. Stuart's favorite horse; killed in action at Chancellorsville.
5. Decatur—Union General Philip Sheridan's warhorse; killed in battle.
6. Nellie Gray—Belonged to Confederate General Fitzhugh Lee; killed in battle at Winchester, Virginia.

⊙ IT'S A FACT

General George A. Custer claimed to have had eleven horses shot out from under him in battle. Other than Custer's word, there is no evidence to support the claim. However, it is known that his favorite horse, Custis Lee, was killed in an accident while being ridden by Custer in a buffalo hunt after the war. Custer shot him by mistake.

UNUSUAL HORSE STORIES FROM
THE CIVIL WAR

★ Dolly, General William T. Sherman's warhorse, was stolen, greatly upsetting the general.

* Baldy, General George Mead's favorite mount, was wounded several times but survived the war.
* Old Sorrel was Stonewall Jackson's warhorse. Old Sorrel's skeleton is preserved at the Virginia Military Institute Museum at Lexington, Virginia.
* Charlie became famous as the horse that threw General Ulysses Grant. Charlie, owned by General Nathaniel Banks, dumped Grant on a downtown street in New Orleans. There were rumors that the general had been drinking.
* Grant was in Cincinnati when a dying man insisted that the general take his favorite horse. Grant named the horse Cincinnati. He later was offered $10,000 in gold for Cincinnati and turned it down.
* Dashing, brave, and handsome, General J.E.B. Stuart enjoyed the modern-day equivalent of rock-star status among female admirers of his era. One smitten belle insisted that the general take her horse, Skylark. Stuart graciously accepted and rode Skylark in several engagements.

RENT-A-NAVY

When civil war broke out in Honduras in 1911, American tycoon Sam "Banana Man" Zemurray requested help from the U.S. Navy to protect his property. He even paid part of the cost of the expedition. Before it was over, U.S. troops helped restore former president Manuel Bonilla to office.

Zemurray was rewarded by Bonilla, receiving large tracts of land suitable for growing bananas and a waiver of taxes for twenty-five years. Zemurray's enterprise eventually became the giant United Fruit Company. It later was revealed that it was Zemurray who financed the civil war against the existing government in the first place.

CAMP DAVID

Camp David was built as a secret retreat for the President and his military planners in World War II. There were no plans for the facility to be used after the war. However, President Dwight Eisenhower enjoyed its solitude and became a frequent visitor. The retreat is named for his grandson. Camp David became a popular getaway for nine successive Presidents.

⊛ IT'S A FACT

Historical reports of Dolley Madison personally cutting the canvas out of the frame in order to save Gilbert Stuart's portrait of George Washington are incorrect. The painting was firmly secured to the wall and far too high for her to reach. As the British closed in on the nation's capital, a gardener brought in a ladder, smashed the heavy frame with an ax, freed the canvas, and handed it to the First Lady.

Reports that Dolley saved the Declaration of Independence also are in error. She only saved her husband's personal papers. Secretary of State James Monroe had his department's critical documents boxed and loaded onto wagons. The documents, including the Declaration of Independence, were transported across the Potomac River to safety. While the nation's capital was in flames, the Declaration of Independence was safely stored at a private home in Leesburg, Virginia.

STONEWALL JACKSON'S VALLEY CAMPAIGN

In the winter of 1861–62, Jackson was sent to Virginia's Shenandoah Valley with 7,600 men to harass federal forces in the region and keep them from joining a spring campaign against the rebel capital at Richmond. After fighting battles at Kernstown and McDowell, Jackson was reinforced by General Richard Ewell's division and General Richard Taylor's Louisiana brigade, bringing the strength of his army to 17,000. At that point, Jackson began one of the most incredible campaigns in the history of warfare:

May 23, 1862—Jackson crossed the Massanutten Mountains and surprised a federal force at Front Royal. He routed the Union troops and took a large number of prisoners.

May 24—At Middletown, he came upon General Nathaniel Banks's supply train and rear guard. Jackson captured the supply train, routed the rear guard, and pursued Banks's army through the night in a rainstorm to Winchester.

May 25—Jackson's swift pursuit prevented Banks from organizing a defense at Winchester. Jackson routed Banks's 10,000-man army and drove it back across the Potomac River to Pennsylvania.

May 26–June 1—There was panic in Washington, D.C., where rumors circulated that Jackson was descending on the nation's capital with 50,000 troops. Instead of marching on Washington, Jackson led his army back down the valley to secure the weapons, munitions, and supplies captured at Middletown.

June 2–June 7—Pursued by three Union armies, Jackson paused to fight engagements at Mt. Carmel and Harrisonburg.

June 8—Trapped between two large armies under the commands of Union generals John Fremont and James Shields, Jackson split his force and attacked both. He hit Fremont first at Cross Keys, halting his advance.

June 9—With Fremont in check, Jackson fell on Shields's army at Port Republic. A vicious battle was under way when Taylor's Brigade made a desperate charge and overran a key Union artillery position, turning the tide of battle. With the defeat of Shields, Jackson slipped away to join Robert E. Lee's forces in the defense of Richmond.

"DEAD ON THE FIELD"

The most casualties inflicted on a regiment in a single Civil War battle took place on July 2, 1864, when the North Carolina 26th Infantry spearheaded a charge to drive Union troops out of the town of Gettysburg. Of the 820 soldiers in the 26th, 86 were killed, 502 wounded, and 120 missing—most of those also killed or wounded.

The following day, when called on to join in Pickett's Charge at Cemetery Ridge, the regiment could muster only 80 men. The greatest percentage of casualties in a single charge was suffered by the 1st Texas Regiment under John Bell Hood at Antietam. Of the 225 men in the unit, 185 were killed or wounded, a casualty rate of 82 percent. Asked where his regiment was after the battle, Hood replied, "Dead on the field."

THE U.S. ARMY IN 1932

When Roosevelt was elected President in 1932, the United States ranked as the sixteenth-largest military in the world, behind countries like Turkey, Poland, Czechoslovakia, Spain, Romania, and Yugoslavia.

THE U.S. ARMY'S K-9 CORPS ANTHEM

From the kennels of the country,
From the homes and firesides too,
We have joined the canine army,
Our nation's work to do.

AMERICAN CODE NAMES FOR JAPANESE AIRCRAFT IN WORLD WAR II

CRAFT	CODE NAME
A5M Navy Mitsubishi fighter	Claude
A6M Mitsubishi fighter (Zero)	Zeke
A7M Navy Reppu fighter	Sam
K127 Army Nakajima fighter	Nate
B5N Nakajima torpedo bomber	Kate
B6N1 Nakajima torpedo bomber	Jill
B7A1 Aichi bomber	Grace

PRESIDENTIAL PROMISES

"And while I am talking to you mothers and
fathers, I give you one more assurance.
I have said this before but I shall say it again
and again and again: Your boys are not going to
be sent into any foreign wars."

President Franklin D. Roosevelt, in a 1939 radio address

"I will never send American boys to fight a war
that Asian boys ought to be fighting."

Lyndon B. Johnson, Presidential candidate in 1960

12 COMMANDS FOR LOADING
AND FIRING A MUSKET

From *Hardee's Rifle and Infantry Tactics* by Colonel William
Hardee, 1856.

1. Load
2. Handle cartridge
3. Tear cartridge
4. Charge cartridge
5. Draw rammer
6. Ram cartridge
7. Return rammer
8. Prime
9. Ready
10. Aim
11. Fire
12. Recover arms

⬛ IT'S A FACT

Colonel Hardee was an instructor at West Point when he wrote his instructional manual. With the outbreak of the Civil War, he joined the Confederate Army and became a general. Hardee's book was used by drill instructors on both sides. In 1863, the U.S. Congress approved $350,000 to purchase copies of the manual for its training officers. Regrettably, for Hardee, he was on the wrong side and never received compensation for his book.

FAMILIES DIVIDED BY THE CIVIL WAR

* Mary Todd Lincoln, wife of President Lincoln, had a brother, three half-brothers, and three brothers-in-law who served in the Confederate Army.
* Union General Philip St. George Cooke had two daughters, both of whom were married to generals—one in the Confederate Army and one in the Union Army. One of St. George's sons-in-law was rebel General J.E.B. Stuart, who ruined his father-in-law's career when he outmaneuvered and defeated his Union cavalry division. St. George was relieved of command as a result of the defeat.
* General George B. McClellan, commander of the Army of the Potomac, was a cousin to Major H. B. McClellan, aide-de-camp to J.E.B. Stuart.
* Union General William Terrill and Confederate General James Terrill were brothers. Both were killed in combat.
* General Edmund Kirby of the Union Army was a cousin to General Edmund Kirby Smith, commander of the Confederate Trans Mississippi Department.

* Lieutenant McKean Buchanan of the Union Navy was killed when his ship was attacked by the Confederate ironclad, CSS *Virginia*. The *Virginia* was commanded by Admiral Franklin Buchanan, his brother.
* Generals Thomas L. Crittenden (Union) and George Crittenden (Confederacy) were brothers.
* Generals John B. McIntosh (Union) and James M. McIntosh (Confederacy) were brothers.
* Union General Edwin Sumner was the son-in-law of rebel General Armistead L. Long.

DATELINE

HEIDELBERG, Germany (December 21, 1945)— General George S. Patton died in an army hospital from chest injuries sustained in an automobile accident on December 9. He was sixty.

UNUSUAL DEATHS OF
8 CIVIL WAR GENERALS

1. Francis Patterson (Union)—Accidentally shot himself.
2. Earl Van Dorn (Confederacy)—Shot in the back by a jealous husband.
3. Joshua Howell (Union)—Fell off his horse.
4. William Baldwin (Confederacy)—Fell off his horse.
5. Lucius Walker (Confederacy)—Killed in a duel.
6. William Nelson (Union)—Murdered by Union General Jefferson C. Davis.
7. Michael Corcoran (Union)—His horse fell on top of him.
8. John Wharton (Confederacy)—He was murdered.

4 CLASSMATES FROM THE WEST POINT
CLASS OF 1846 KILLED IN COMBAT

1. General Jesse Reno, Union, killed at South Mountain
2. General Thomas (Stonewall) Jackson, Confederacy, killed at Chancellorsville
3. General A. P. Hill, Confederacy, killed at Petersburg
4. General John Adams, Confederacy, killed in Virginia

MACARTHUR'S KOREAN WAR STRATEGY

In the winter of 1951, hundreds of thousands of Red Chinese soldiers poured across the Yalu River into North Korea and overwhelmed United Nations forces under the command of General Douglas MacArthur. As his badly outmanned army was driven into retreat, a frantic MacArthur proposed the following strategy:

1. Drop thirty to fifty atom bombs on Chinese bases and staging points in Manchuria.
2. Land 500,000 Chinese Nationalist troops from Formosa behind enemy lines, backed by two divisions of U.S. Marines. This force would cut supply lines and cut off the attacking Red Chinese Army.
3. After defeating the Red Chinese in Korea, he proposed laying down a belt of radioactive cobalt along the Yalu River between Korea and Manchuria to prevent future invasions.

"THEY WON'T ESCAPE THIS TIME!"

When the Red Chinese Army invaded North Korea, the 1st Marine Division was trapped forty miles behind enemy lines. The unit, accompanied by elements of the Republic of Korea Capital Division and the 3rd and 8th U.S. Army divisions, fought their way to the Port of Hungnam, where they were evacuated. A famous quotation emerged as the Marines hacked their way through hordes of Chinese troops and Colonel Lewis B. "Chesty" Puller said to his regiment: "The enemy is in front of us, behind us, to the left of us, and to the right of us. They won't escape this time!"

THE KAMIKAZES OF VIETNAM

The Japanese kamikaze pilots of World War II and radical Muslim terrorists of the Middle East are not the only zealots to sacrifice their lives. At Fire Base Russell in Vietnam, Vietcong lashed dynamite to their bodies and threw themselves on barbed wire protecting the perimeter of the base, opening gaps through which their comrades could attack.

◉ IT'S A FACT

In 1951, the Chinese Nationalists on Formosa had the fifth-largest army in the world. While MacArthur wanted to bring the Nationalists into the war, President Truman feared by doing so the Soviet Union would enter the conflict, creating a world war.

THE MY LAI MASSACRE

On March 16, 1968, helicopters landed near the village of My Lai, Vietnam, and a platoon from Company C of the 11th Infantry Brigade poured out with their M16 automatic rifles loaded and ready. Some six hours later, as many as 567 villagers were dead—most of them old men, women, and children. The massacre at My Lai was the worst atrocity of a war filled with atrocities on both sides. The platoon was under the command of Lieutenant William Calley, who, three years later, was convicted of murder and sentenced to life in prison for his role in the massacre. How could such an event happen?

1. Company C had been in Vietnam just three months and had lost almost half of its 190 men to booby traps and ambushes by the Vietcong. The men were bent on revenge.
2. Army intelligence had erroneously identified My Lai as a base for the 48th Battalion of the Vietcong.
3. Lt. Calley was under orders from his superior, Captain Ernest Medina, to "clean it [the village] out."
4. When there was no Vietcong resistance, Lt. Calley began herding villagers into groups and ordered them shot. Those who would not come out of their hooches were blown up by grenades tossed inside.
5. Little–reported was the fact that several soldiers in the platoon defied orders and refused to participate in the massacre. The only U.S. casualty that day was a private who shot himself in the foot so that he did not have to take part in the killing.
6. The event was recorded on film by army photographer Ronald Haeberle, who became a star witness for the prosecution.

7. Several soldiers were tried for murder, including Captain Medina, but only Calley was found guilty.

BATTLE HYMN OF LT. CALLEY

Within three days after William Calley's conviction, Plantation Records had sold 202,000 copies of the song "The Battle Hymn of Lieutenant Calley." That week, Viking Press announced it was paying Calley $100,000 for his story. A flood of mail at the White House ran a hundred to one calling for Calley's release. President Nixon responded by ordering Calley removed from prison and placed under house arrest. Under pressure from the Pentagon, Nixon later reversed the decision, and Calley spent several years in the Fort Benning stockade before being paroled.

> *My name is William Calley, I'm a soldier of this land,*
> *I've tried to do my duty and to gain the upper hand*
> *But they've made me out a villain,*
> *they have stamped me with a brand,*
> *As we go marching on.*

First verse of "The Battle Hymn of Lt. Calley"

❧ NOTABLE QUOTE

"I told them to hell with this, I'm not doing it. This is point-blank murder."

Sergeant Michael Bernhardt on the My Lai massacre

THE BATTLE FOR HAMBURGER HILL

It was not a major battle. But no single engagement in the Vietnam War had more influence on its eventual outcome than the Battle for Hamburger Hill. It took place in western Vietnam near the Laotian border where a low mountain looks down on the A Shau Valley, a major corridor for enemy infiltration.

Nine U.S. battalions were sent to drive the Vietcong off the mountain and stop the flow of men and materials from North Vietnam. Two attempts to storm the position were thrown back by what General Melvin Zais called "a hornet's nest" of resistance.

U.S. artillery rained more than 2,000 shells on the enemy position, prompting the Americans to nickname it "Hamburger Hill." A third infantry assault was driven back by rifle fire and grenades. The Air Force was called in to pound the summit with 155 bombing runs.

For ten days, American forces tried to take Hamburger Hill. Finally, on the tenth assault, 1,400 troops stormed the position and planted the American flag on its crest. The cost was 442 casualties—70 killed and 372 wounded. General Zais called it "a great victory by a gutsy bunch of guys."

One week later, U.S. Army brass at the Pentagon issued orders to abandon the position because "it has no strategic value." The American public, having followed daily reports of the battle, was outraged. More significantly, Congress was outraged. Many who had supported the war, including several Republican senators, demanded that President Richard Nixon begin withdrawing American troops from Vietnam.

Thus Hamburger Hill became a tipping point—signaling the beginning of the end of U.S. involvement in Vietnam.

DATELINE

WASHINGTON, D.C. (April 7, 1978)——President Carter announced he would defer production of a neutron bomb. The bomb was designed to emit deadly doses of radiation while causing only minor damage to structures. European nations had expressed strong opposition to development of such a weapon.

FACT OR FICTION

PRESIDENT FRANKLIN ROOSEVELT ORDERED THE ASSASSINATION OF AN ENEMY COMMANDER

THE STORY: Upon receiving intelligence on the flight plans of Japanese Admiral Isoroku Yamamoto, Roosevelt ordered his plane shot down.

THE FACTS: Despite denials at the time, the story is true. Yamamoto was the man who masterminded the attack on Pearl Harbor. He also was commander of the Japanese fleet at the Battle of Midway. Shortly after his defeat at Midway, U.S. code-breakers learned of Yamamoto's flight plans. With Roosevelt's approval, American P-38s sought out his aircraft and, on April 18, 1943, shot it down over the Shortland Islands, killing Japan's most famous admiral.

DATELINE

WASHINGTON, D.C. (November 14, 1909)——
President Taft selected Pearl Harbor as the site for the prin-
cipal U.S. military base in the Pacific, ending a dispute
between the Army and Navy brass over the location. The
Navy wanted the base in the Philippines.

WHAT A WORLD WAR II GI
CARRIED INTO BATTLE

The fully equipped American infantryman in World War II
was as much a beast of burden as he was a warrior.
According to the Quartermaster Corps, the average GI
lugged 84.3 pounds when he was on the march. He carried:

His uniform	Ammunition bandoleer
Steel helmet	Backpack
Helmet line	Extra clothing
M1 rifle	Writing paper/letters
A knife	Extra socks/underwear
Canteen	A poncho
Pick-shovel	Primacord fuses
Bayonet	Mess kit
First-aid pouch	Zippo lighter
Web cartridge belt	Canned ham and eggs
Hand grenades	C and K rations
Gas mask	

In addition the GI had to carry part of his outfit's communal weaponry—a Browning automatic rifle or its tripod, a light or heavy machine gun or the tripod, a 60- or 81-millimeter mortar or its base. The most important item in a GI's pack was a clean pair of socks. The least useful item—a gas mask, which often was the first thing discarded.

DATELINE

HAMPTON ROADS, Virginia (November 14, 1910)— A Curtiss biplane piloted by Eugene Ely took off from a ramp constructed on the deck of the USS *Birmingham,* becoming the first aircraft launched from a ship.

THE ABC-1 PLAN

Eleven months before Pearl Harbor, British and American representatives met in Washington, D.C., to plan strategy *if* the United States entered the war. The planners met fourteen times between January and March 1941. The strategy that was approved called for the defeat of Germany and Italy first and stabilization of the Mediterranean Theater before any offensive action was taken against the Japanese in the Pacific. It was called the ABC-1 Plan. The Japanese surprise attack on Pearl Harbor, Dec. 7, 1941, forced the United States to abandon the plan and commit to a major war in the Pacific.

⬡ IT'S A FACT

* On paper there were 138,069 men in the U.S. military in 1932. In reality, only about 30,000 were available for actual military duty. The others were assigned to desk work, guarding the Mexican border, or protecting U.S. possessions overseas.

* The Secretaries of State, the Army, and the Navy were all located on the same floor in the old Executive Office Building.

* General Douglas MacArthur was the nation's only four-star general. There were no three-star generals.

* As Army Chief of Staff, MacArthur rode around Washington, D.C., in the army's only limousine.

* For a time, MacArthur did not have a phone on his desk.

* MacArthur had only one aide—a young major named Dwight Eisenhower.

* Although MacArthur had a limousine, when it was necessary for Eisenhower to get around town, he had to fill out a requisition form for trolley tickets.

* Eisenhower came close to resigning his commission because of boredom. He later admitted he spent his time reading adventure pulp magazines.

* Also assigned to duty in Washington, D.C., was Major George Patton. He spent his time playing polo, skeet-shooting, steeplechasing, foxhunting, and flying. Patton was rich. Eisenhower was not.

AXIS SALLY

An aspiring actress, Mildred Elizabeth Gillars was an American living in Berlin when World War II began. Her lover, Max Koischwitz, convinced her to do a radio show aimed at undermining the morale of American GIs. She played music and talked in a sultry voice, questioning the role of American soldiers in a European war and describing how the men back home were seducing the wives and sweethearts of the troops overseas. Nicknamed "Axis Sally," her show became more popular with the GIs than the official U.S. Army station, due in part to her playing of the song "Lili Marlene," which was a favorite of Allied troops as well as the Germans. She was convicted of treason in 1949 and received a pardon in 1961.

ARTIFICIAL MOONLIGHT

In Normandy, British and American forces discovered they could light a battlefield at night by aiming searchlights at low clouds. Under ideal weather conditions, the reflection would light an enemy position miles away. While Allied forces experimented with this concept, the Germans used it with success at the outset of the Battle of the Bulge.

⬟ IT'S A FACT

The first Civil War ambulances made their appearance at the Battle of Shiloh. A fully stocked Union medical wagon contained first-aid kits, fifty-two medicines, condensed milk, sponges, tourniquets, and silk thread for sewing wounds.

THE AMERICAL DIVISION

The Americal was the only U.S. division in World War II to have a name and not a number. The 164th Infantry Regiment from the division participated in the invasion of Guadalcanal, becoming one of the first American units to be involved in an offensive action in World War II. In addition to Guadalcanal, the division was in the following campaigns: the Solomons, Southern Philippines, Leyte, and the occupation of Japan. The unit was inactivated Dec. 12, 1945, at Fort Lawton, Washington.

FROM HERO TO INFAMY:
THE STORY OF DANIEL SHAYS

Seldom explored is the tragic story of Daniel Shays, the man who led America's second revolution. An ordinary farmer, Shays distinguished himself as a captain in the Continental Army in the War for Independence, fighting bravely at Bunker Hill, Ticonderoga, and Saratoga. Following the conflict, he and his fellow farmers in Western Massachusetts were burdened by taxes imposed to pay for the war.

While many of his neighbors were ready to take up arms and challenge the authorities, Shays preached restraint. But, in 1786, when taxes were increased once more and the courts began seizing farms, the farmers formed a loose-knit rebel army called the Regulators. With Shays as their somewhat reluctant leader, the Regulators prevented courts from meeting and protected their properties with arms.

In 1787, the Regulators marched on Springfield and prevented the State Supreme Court from meeting. Later, when the rebels tried to break into the Springfield arsenal, they were routed by the regular army. Eight Regulators were arrested and two hanged. Shays escaped and fled to Vermont.

The rebellion had a positive effect by bringing widespread attention to the plight of the farmers, forcing Congress to reduce taxes. Shays received a pardon. He lived out his life in obscurity in New York City, never returning to his farm or Massachusetts, where he was held in contempt by many of his neighbors.

BATTLE BETWEEN CAVALRY AND GUNBOATS

In the spring of 1864, one of the most unusual engagements of the Civil War took place when Confederate cavalry battled Union gunboats on the Red River in Louisiana. Using light field artillery that could be transported along the banks of the river, the rebels repeatedly ambushed Union Admiral David Porter's fleet.

In one attack on the admiral's flagship, the *Cricket,* Porter noted that the vessel took thirty-eight artillery hits in a matter of minutes. With most of his crew dead or wounded and the gunboat drifting out of control, Porter personally took the wheel and steered it beyond the range of rebel guns. A veteran of many battles, Porter reported in his memoirs, "This was the heaviest fire I ever witnessed."

In a series of close-quarter battles over several weeks, rebel cavalry sank three ironclad gunboats and seven transports. It was the costliest single engagement of the war for the Union Navy.

⬟ IT'S A FACT

President George W. Bush was faulted for waiting seven minutes before reacting to news of the September 11, 2001, terrorist attack on the Twin Towers. When Roosevelt was informed of the attack on Pearl Harbor, he sat in silence for twenty-two minutes, collecting his thoughts, before reaching for a telephone and calling aides to the White House.

THE ACCIDENTAL BOMBING THAT COST
COUNTLESS CIVILIAN LIVES

Until August 1940, Germany and Great Britain limited their air strikes to military targets and carefully avoided bombing civilian population centers. But on the night of August 24, ten German aircraft became lost and accidentally bombed London, killing civilians.

The next night, the British retaliated, sending eighty planes to bomb Berlin. That raid provoked the Germans to start regular bombing raids on London beginning Sept. 6, 1940. The United States began bombing runs over Berlin early in 1944, with devastating results for the bomber crews. In just one raid, on March 6, the U.S. 8th Air Force lost sixty-nine planes over Berlin.

On February 3, 1945, 1,000 American bombers devastated Berlin, killing an estimated 25,000 civilians and destroying much of the city. But the deadliest raid of the war took place February 13–14, when 450 U.S. B-17s and 550 British RAF bombers pounded the German city of Dresden to rubble, killing 130,000.

By the end of the war an estimated 250,000 German and

52,000 English civilians were killed in bombing raids. When the last bomb fell on Berlin on April 21, 1945, 6,340 acres in the heart of the city had been destroyed.

GENERALS WHO BECAME PRESIDENT

George Washington
Andrew Jackson
William Henry Harrison
Zachary Taylor
Andrew Johnson
Ulysses S. Grant
Rutherford B. Hayes
James A. Garfield
Benjamin Harrison
Dwight D. Eisenhower

MILITARY RECORDS OF U.S. PRESIDENTS

GEORGE WASHINGTON—Commander of the Continental Army in the American Revolution. Defeated Cornwallis at Yorktown.

JAMES MADISON—Became the only sitting President to be involved in an actual battle, when British attacked Washington, D.C., in the War of 1812.

JAMES MONROE—A junior officer under Washington in the American Revolution, he was wounded in the shoulder by a musket ball at the Battle of Trenton.

ANDREW JACKSON—Fought in wars from the American Revolution to the Creek and Seminole Indian Wars in the 1820s. Commanding general at the Battle of New

Orleans, where he orchestrated a brilliant victory against a superior British force.

WILLIAM HENRY HARRISON—Earned his reputation by defeating an Indian alliance at the Tippecanoe River in 1811. In the War of 1812, defeated the British at the Battle of the Thames.

ZACHARY TAYLOR—Fought in the War of 1812, the Black Hawk War, and the Seminole War. In the War with Mexico, as commander of U.S. forces in Northern Mexico, defeated Santa Anna's army at Buena Vista.

ABRAHAM LINCOLN—A militia captain in the Black Hawk War, his unit never saw combat.

ANDREW JOHNSON—Lincoln appointed him military governor of occupied Tennessee with the rank of general.

ULYSSES S. GRANT—Given command of all Union forces in 1864, he pursued a war of attrition, forcing a weakened Southern army to surrender at Appomattox in 1865, effectively ending the Civil War.

RUTHERFORD B. HAYES—In the Civil War, rose from major to major general. Fearless in battle, he was wounded several times.

JAMES A. GARFIELD—Rose to the rank of major general in the Union Army and distinguished himself in several important battles—most notably at Chickamauga.

GROVER CLEVELAND—During the Civil War, he paid a Polish immigrant $150 to take his place in the draft.

BENJAMIN HARRISON—A brigadier general, he compiled a distinguished record in the Civil War.

WILLIAM MCKINLEY—Served in the Civil War. Enlisted as a private in the Union Army and rose to the rank of major.

THEODORE ROOSEVELT—When the U.S. declared war against Spain, Roosevelt resigned as Assistant Secretary of the Navy, formed a cavalry regiment, accepted a commission as a lieutenant-colonel, and saw action in Cuba.

WILLIAM HOWARD TAFT—Served as Secretary of War under Theodore Roosevelt.

FRANKLIN D. ROOSEVELT—He was Assistant Secretary of the Navy before becoming President and commander in chief in World War II.

HARRY S. TRUMAN—Served as a captain of artillery in Europe in World War I.

DWIGHT D. EISENHOWER—Commander in chief of allied forces in World War II.

JOHN F. KENNEDY—Commander of Navy PT Boat 109 in World War II. His was the only PT boat to be rammed and sunk in the war. Thanks to the influence of his father, Kennedy narrowly escaped court-martial and emerged a hero.

LYNDON B. JOHNSON—A U.S. representative at the outbreak of World War II, he sought a commission and went on a bomb run to boost his political resumé.

RICHARD M. NIXON—Joined the navy in 1942 and was commissioned a lieutenant. Served as an air transport officer in the backwash of the Pacific Theater.

GERALD FORD—Served as a navy officer in the Pacific in World War II.

JIMMY CARTER—Graduated 59th in a class of 820 at Annapolis. Studied nuclear physics while training for submarine service. Intended to become a career officer but had to resign and return home to run the family farm in Georgia.

RONALD REAGAN—Enlisted in World War II, but the only shooting he did was to make propaganda films for the U.S. Army.

GEORGE H. W. BUSH—At eighteen, the youngest combat pilot in the U.S. Navy in World War II. Narrowly escaped death when his craft was shot down in the Pacific Theater.

GEORGE W. BUSH—Served in the Air National Guard and remained stateside during the War in Vietnam.

⊛ IT'S A FACT

In later years, Eisenhower admitted that among his preferred reading materials were the following pulp magazines: *Two-Gun Western, Western Story, Thrilling Western,* and *Cowboy Short Stories.*

---

6 PRO ATHLETES KILLED IN ACTION

EDDIE GRANT—Third baseman for the Philadelphia Phillies, Cincinnati Reds, and New York Giants. Volunteered for duty in 1917. Killed in an artillery bombardment as he led his unit in an attempt to rescue the famous "Lost Battalion."

ELMER GEDEON—An outfielder for the Washington Senators. Gedeon was piloting a B-26 bomber over France in 1944 when his plane was shot down. He died in the crash.

JACK LUMMUS—An all-star end for the New York Giants football team, he was killed in action on Iwo Jima. Lummus was posthumously awarded the Medal of Honor.

DON STEINBRUNNER—He was an offensive lineman for the Cleveland Browns in the 1950s. Steinbrunner became a navigator in the Air Force and was killed when his aircraft was shot down over Vietnam in 1967.

BOB KALSU—An offensive guard for the Buffalo Bills, Kalsu joined the Army in 1969. He was killed in an artillery bombardment in Vietnam in 1970.

PAT TILLMAN—Turned his back on a $3.6-million contract as safety for the Arizona Cardinals to join the Army following the terrorist attacks of September 11, 2001. He was killed on patrol in eastern Afghanistan in April 2004.

DATELINE

WASHINGTON, D.C. (December 7, 1978)——A ruling by a U.S. appeals court required the U.S. Defense Department to accept homosexuals in the military unless "some reasonable explanation can be offered for their exclusion."

 IT'S A FACT

In 1971, when John Wayne was sixty-three, he attended the inauguration of California Governor Ronald Reagan. Spotting a group of Vietnam War protesters waving a Vietcong flag, he yelled, "You dirty bastards," and plunged into the crowd with fists flying. The police had to break up the fight. One of the protesters insisted that Wayne be arrested. The police refused to file charges but threatened to jail the protester if he persisted, and the matter was dropped.

FOUR WORLD WAR II HEROES
WHO NEVER FIRED A SHOT

In February of 1943, a torpedo struck the hull of the army transport vessel *Dorchester* in the North Atlantic. As the ship was sinking, four chaplains took off their life jackets and gave them to soldiers. The four went down with the ship. The U.S. Postal Service later issued a stamp in their honor. The four chaplains were:

Clark V. Poling, Protestant
John P. Washington, Roman Catholic
Alexander D. Goode, Jewish
George L. Fox, Protestant

THE FORGOTTEN ISLAND BATTLE
OF WORLD WAR II

The Pacific islands of Iwo Jima, Guadalcanal, Luzon, and Okinawa are well known because of the bitter fighting that took place there. However, one of the most vicious battles of the war took place on an island far removed from the South Pacific.

It happened on tiny Attu, one of the westernmost islands of the Aleutian chain that stretches from Alaska to near the Asian mainland. The Japanese seized Attu on June 7, 1942. By the time the U.S. 7th Infantry Division landed there in May 1943 to take back the island, more than 2,400 Japanese troops were dug in on terrain ideally suited for defense.

The battle raged for eighteen days before a superior American force finally destroyed the Japanese garrison. So ferocious was the fighting that only thirty Japanese soldiers were taken alive. American losses were 550 killed and 1,150 wounded.

ROBERT E. LEE'S RELATIONSHIP TO GEORGE WASHINGTON

In 1759, George Washington, then twenty-seven, married a wealthy widow named Martha Parke Custis, who had two children—John and Martha Parke. John Parke was killed in the Revolutionary War. He was survived by four children, two of whom were adopted by George Washington. One of those children was George Washington Parke Custis. When Washington died in 1799, this adopted son moved from Mount Vernon and built Arlington overlooking the Potomac River. He had four children, but only one survived to adulthood. She was Mary Anne Randolph Custis. It was this granddaughter of Washington, through adoption, who married Robert E. Lee. Washington, the father of the country, never fathered a child.

◆ **IT'S A FACT**

Robert E. Lee was related to two other presidents. James Madison and Zachary Taylor were his cousins. His father was "Light Horse" Harry Lee, a member of the Continental Congress and a war hero in the American Revolution.

HOW LONG SOME FAMOUS BATTLES LASTED

YORKTOWN (1781)—Thirteen days before
Cornwallis surrendered to Washington.

BATTLE OF NEW ORLEANS (1815)—Lasted six
hours.

BOMBARDMENT OF FORT SUMTER
(1861)—Lasted thirty-four hours.

BATTLE FOR RICHMOND, VA. (1862)—Lasted
seven days.

BATTLE OF MIDWAY (1942)—Lasted two days.

SIEGE OF PORT HUDSON (1863)—Lasted 48
days.

SIEGE OF VICKSBURG (1863)—Lasted 49 days.

GUADALCANAL (1942–43)—Lasted six months.

NORMANDY INVASION (1944)—Lasted 76 days.

BATTLE OF THE BULGE (1944)—Lasted 41 days.

BATTLE OF HEARTBREAK RIDGE, KOREA
(1951)—Lasted 37 days.

OPERATION DESERT STORM, IRAQ (1990)—
Lasted three days.

OPERATION IRAQI FREEDOM (2003)—Lasted
twenty-one days from invasion day until the fall
of Baghdad. Guerrilla warfare is ongoing.

THE WATERMELON WAR

In 1856, President Franklin Pierce dispatched troops to
what is now Panama to put down riots and protect the

Atlantic–Pacific Railroad that crossed the isthmus. The uprising was triggered when an American named Jack Oliver stole a slice of watermelon from a street vendor. An argument between Oliver and the vendor escalated into a brawl and then a riot. A general uprising threatened the vital rail line before American troops arrived to restore order. The incident became known as the Watermelon War.

WHEN POLITICS OUTRANKED MILITARY STRATEGY

In the early weeks of the Mexican War, General Zachary Taylor won a series of brilliant victories in Northern Mexico. Because this was the first war reported by telegraph, stories appeared daily in U.S. newspapers praising Taylor's triumphs.

After capturing Monterey and routing Santa Anna's 15,000-man army at Buena Vista, he might have marched on Mexico City and quickly ended the war. But President James K. Polk had other ideas. Polk reassigned half of Taylor's troops to General Winfield Scott for a coastal invasion of Mexico.

The decision had little to do with military strategy. Because of Taylor's sudden popularity, he was being mentioned as a Presidential candidate on the Whig Party ticket. Polk, a Democrat, wanted Scott to succeed him in the White House. Scott captured Mexico City and emerged the hero of the Mexican War. But it was Taylor who became President.

HOW A COMPUTER GLITCH ALMOST
LAUNCHED A NUCLEAR WAR—TWICE

June 3, 1980, was another ordinary day for most Americans, but not for those manning the Strategic Air Command computers at Omaha, Nebraska. The computers indicated that the United States was under attack by missiles launched from submarines. An alarm went out and within minutes more than 100 SAC B-52 aircraft loaded with nuclear bombs were headed for the Soviet Union. SAC officials quickly discovered that the computers had made a mistake and called off the attack. Three days later the same thing happened again. This time SAC investigators discovered the problem. It was a faulty computer chip that cost forty-six cents.

WORDS OF WISDOM FROM
"OL' BLOOD 'N' GUTS"

"Our blood and his guts" was the way the men under George Patton put it. If a reporter was around, Patton was never at a loss for a one-liner. Among those attributed to him:

* "A pint of sweat will save a gallon of blood."
* "In war, just as in loving, you've got to keep on shoving."
* "To win battles, you do not beat weapons. You beat the soul of the enemy man."
* "Wars may be fought with weapons, but they are won by men."

* "The most vital quality a soldier can possess is self-confidence—utter, complete, and bumptious."
* "Never tell people how to do things. Tell them what to do and they will surprise you with their ingenuity."
* "Untutored courage is useless in the face of educated bullets."
* "Take calculated risk. That's quite different from being rash."
* "Attack weakness. Then hold them by the nose and kick them in the pants."
* "There's one thing you men will be able to say when you get home. You can thank God for it. Thirty years from now, when you are sitting around the fireside with your grandson on your knee and he asks what you did in the great World War Two, you won't have to say, 'I shoveled crap in Louisiana.'"

THE FIRST U.S. JET ACE

On May 20, 1951, Captain James Jabara became the first American jet ace when he shot down his fifth and sixth MIG fighters over Korea. Jabara also was an ace in World War II.

⊙ IT'S A FACT

Because there was no code name for the stripped-down MXY7 Japanese suicide plane, U.S. sailors referred to it simply as the Gizmo. Later the plane was given the code name Baka, the Japanese word for "fool."

2 WHO OPPOSED DROPPING THE A-BOMB

GENERAL DWIGHT EISENHOWER, Supreme Allied Commander: "Japan was defeated....I thought our country should avoid shocking world opinion by the use of a weapon whose employment, I thought, was no longer mandatory as a measure to save American lives."

ADMIRAL WILLIAM B. LEAHY, chief of staff and chairman of the Joint Chiefs of Staff: "I don't think the bomb will ever go off," a skeptical Leahy said before the event. Afterward he said, "The Japanese were defeated and ready to surrender.... We adopted an ethical standard common to the barbarians of the Dark Ages."

PRESIDENT HARRY TRUMAN: "Leahy never got over being wrong about the bomb going off."

WHY "DUKE" NEVER SERVED IN THE MILITARY

1. He had a perforated eardrum.
2. He had four children.

Little known is the fact that when John Wayne finished high school, he applied for admission to the U.S. Naval Academy at Annapolis but was turned down. Disappointed, he enrolled at USC, where he played football and worked part-time for a movie studio as a grunt, lifting boxes and setting up props. By the start of World War II, he had become a major movie star. Exempted from military service, he made numerous movies portraying war heroes. In an interview near the end of his career, Wayne made reference to his rejection by the Naval Academy and noted: "If they had accepted me, I'd probably be a retired admiral by now." Although Wayne never became an admiral, he portrayed one in the movie *In Harm's Way*.

OTHER MOVIE ACTORS WHO FLUNKED THE PHYSICAL

Gary Cooper (displaced hip)
Frank Sinatra (punctured eardrum)
Jackie Gleason (overweight)
Marlon Brando (bad knees)
Dean Martin (hernia)
Gregory Peck (ruptured vertebrae)
Cliff Robertson (poor eyesight)

HOW THE U.S. NAVY ALMOST TORPEDOED A PRESIDENT

On November 14, 1943, the destroyer *William D. Porter* was engaged in practice maneuvers when the crew inadvertently fired a live torpedo toward the battleship *Iowa*. Panic ensued aboard both vessels as the *Iowa*'s skipper desperately made a high-speed turn to avoid the torpedo. The errant torpedo narrowly missed the *Iowa* and exploded in the ship's wake, detonated by the force of the turbulent waters churned up by the movement of the ship.

The quick action by the *Iowa*'s skipper not only saved his ship but possibly the lives of several VIP passengers. On board the *Iowa* were President Franklin D. Roosevelt and the Joint Chiefs of Staff, en route to Cairo, Egypt, for a top-secret meeting with Winston Churchill and Chiang Kai-shek.

FACT OR FICTION?

WILLIAM RANDOLPH HEARST STARTED THE SPANISH–AMERICAN WAR

THE STORY: As the owner of a chain of newspapers in the 1890s, William Randolph Hearst was the most powerful newsman in the United States. Convinced that war was inevitable in Cuba, Hearst sent famous artist Frederic Remington to Havana to sketch the action for his newspapers.

Upon arriving there, Remington cabled Hearst: "There is no trouble here. There will be no war. I wish to return." Hearst wired back: "You furnish the pictures and I'll furnish the war." According to the legend, Hearst used his newspapers to create enough pro-war sentiment to actually start the conflict.

THE FACTS: The Hearst newspapers, indeed, saber-rattled for war, but there is no evidence that Hearst himself ever cabled Remington promising to provide one for him to sketch. In fact, Hearst denied the rumor.

The story was published in the memoirs of James Creelman, several years after the war. Creelman was a former reporter who worked for Hearst. No evidence was ever produced to substantiate the claim.

LAST OF THE "MOUNTAIN DEVILS"

Hiro Onoda became a Japanese soldier when he was eighteen. In 1945 he was on Lubang Island in the Philippines when United States troops overran it. Most of the Japanese there were captured or killed. Onoda was in a group that fled into the mountains and hid out.

When the war ended, the U.S. and Japanese governments knew that holdouts remained on the island. Expeditions were sent to find them; leaflets were dropped, urging them to surrender, without success.

For years the holdouts survived by raiding native villages, earning the nickname "Mountain Devils." As years passed, Onoda's comrades died off from disease and exposure, until only he remained.

In 1974, a university student named Norio Suzuki spent months on Lubang Island looking for survivors. While Suzuki was drinking from a stream, Onoda approached him. Informed the war was long over, Onoda still refused to surrender unless ordered to do so by his commanding officer.

Suzuki returned to Japan, found the officer, and brought him back to the island. Twenty-nine years after hostilities ended, Onoda returned to Japan, at age fifty-two. He was greeted by a crowd of 4,000 at the airport. His memoirs became a bestselling book in Japan. He used the money to retire to Brazil, where he bought a 2,800-acre ranch and lived out his life in quiet solitude.

DATELINE

HUFFMAN PRAIRIE, Ohio (September 20, 1904)—The Wright brothers demonstrated the capabilities of their latest flying machine, *Flyer II*. Orville Wright expressed his disappointment that U.S. Army officials turned down an offer to produce their airplane for military use. The brothers would sign a contract with France before the U.S. Army finally showed interest.

NUCLEAR BOMB ACCIDENTS

1. In 1980 a workman at a Titan II silo in Arkansas dropped a tool that punctured a missile housing. It triggered an explosion that blew the top off the silo and hurled a nuclear warhead 600 feet into the air. Fortunately, the warhead failed to explode.

2. On January 21, 1968, a fire broke out on a B-52 off the coast of Greenland. Six crewmen parachuted to safety but the copilot could not get out and was killed when the plane plunged through the ice into the ocean. Four hydrogen bombs were retrieved from the wreckage.

3. In 1966, a B-52 carrying four nuclear bombs crashed off the coast of Spain. Although three of the bombs were quickly recovered, a twenty-megaton bomb remained lost. A fleet of thirty-three ships spent eight weeks searching for it before the crew of a midget sub finally located the bomb, and it was removed without incident.

4. In 1961, a B-52 crew accidentally dropped two twenty-four-megaton bombs while flying over North Carolina. The bombs were located on a farm and removed.

5. In 1958 a nuclear bomb was accidentally dropped as a B-47 flew over Mars Bluff, South Carolina. The bomb damaged several houses and a church before coming to rest in a family's vegetable garden.

6. In 1956 a U.S. aircraft crashed into a storage building at an airport near Cambridge, England. Jet fuel from the plane ignited. Firefighters frantically fought the blaze and subdued it before it could reach vital contents in the building—three nuclear bombs.

BEYOND THE CALL OF DUTY

In Peking, China, during the Boxer Rebellion in 1900, U.S. Marines were pinned down in a defensive position under attack by hordes of Chinese. As the battle raged, it became apparent that one flank was vulnerable. The Marines managed to hold the position but realized they must build a barricade during the night or be overrun the next day.

Private Daniel Daly volunteered to crawl along the Tartar Wall some 100 yards distance and hold back any encroaching Chinese while the barricade was being constructed. That night, as the Chinese tried to infiltrate along the wall, Daly cut them down with rifle fire. At times he had to fight with his bayonet and the butt of his rifle. But not one Chinese got past him. At dawn Daly still held his position, surrounded by the bodies of those he had killed.

Daly was awarded the Medal of Honor. He later received a second one during a campaign in Haiti and was nominated for a third.

❧ NOTABLE QUOTE

"Some commanders were anxious to gain as much ground as possible . . . . It was like a child who had been given a toy that he is much interested in and he knows that in a day or two it is going to be taken away from him and he wants to use that toy up to the handle while he has it."

General John Sherburne in testimony to a Congressional committee

FACT OR FICTION?

THE JAPANESE WERE PLANNING TO SURRENDER WHEN THE A-BOMBS FELL

THE STORY: The Japanese cabinet had already decided to surrender, and dropping atomic bombs on Hiroshima and Nagasaki was unnecessary.

THE FACTS: Entries in President Harry Truman's journal indicate that Emperor Hirohito was prepared to end the war (but not surrender) in June 1945, two months before the A-bombs were dropped. The Allies responded by sending a telegram to the Japanese government demanding that it surrender forthwith. Japanese officials replied that they would reserve comment on the ultimatum pending deliberations by the Imperial government. But that is not how it was interpreted.

Unfortunately, the Japanese News Agency issued the reply in English and misinterpreted the word *mokusatsu*. Instead of "to reserve comment," the translation became "to ignore." President Harry Truman considered this an outright rejection of his ultimatum.

Truman became even more incensed when he learned the Japanese were trying to negotiate a separate peace settlement with the Soviet Union if the Soviets would not invade Manchuria.

Truman did not trust Soviet Premier Joseph Stalin or the Japanese. He wanted an unconditional surrender by Japan to the United States. When the Japanese did not respond, Truman decided to end the war quickly, before Japan and the Soviets reached an agreement.

The first atom bomb fell on Hiroshima on August 6,

1945, killing 70,000. On August 8, the Soviet Union began an invasion of Manchuria. On August 9, the Japanese cabinet and the emperor finally agreed to start the surrender process but did not communicate their intent to the United States. That same day, a second A-bomb fell on Nagasaki, killing 45,000.

Japan finally announced its surrender August 14. The official ceremony of surrender took place September 2. In fact, the Japanese had opportunities to surrender before Truman authorized the use of atom bombs. Regrettably, Japanese leaders were intent on reaching a cease-fire instead of a surrender, a condition unacceptable to Truman.

Some historians have speculated that in addition to quickly ending the war, Truman wanted to demonstrate the power of nuclear weapons to the Soviet Union as a warning against expansion in the Far East.

ANYONE WHO DID NOT GET A MEDAL?

In the 1984 invasion of the Island of Grenada, 8,600 medals were awarded to United States military personnel. Noteworthy is the fact that only 7,000 troops participated in the campaign.

✎ NOTABLE QUOTE

"Those clodhoppers will not attack us."

Colonel Johann Rall the day before the
Battle of Trenton

FACT OR FICTION?

FRANKLIN ROOSEVELT KNEW THE JAPANESE WERE GOING TO ATTACK PEARL HARBOR

THE STORY: On December 7, 1941, Japanese warplanes attacked the U.S. military base at Pearl Harbor. In less than two hours, 12 warships were sunk or damaged, some 200 aircraft destroyed on the ground, and 2,403 soldiers and sailors killed. The smoke had hardly cleared when speculation began that President Roosevelt knew the attack was coming and allowed it to happen to draw the United States into the war.

THE FACTS: On November 27, eleven days before the attack, General George Marshall sent the following message to the commander at Pearl Harbor: "Hostile action possible at any moment." If Marshall knew an attack was imminent, there can be little doubt that Roosevelt also knew. What neither knew was the date. That was a closely held secret, known by only a few top Japanese military planners.

By the end of World War II there were no less than seven Pearl Harbor investigations by Congress and the U.S. military. The inquiries revealed that the U.S. had broken the Japanese diplomatic code, nicknamed "Purple," more than two years before the attack. Although there was never a message clearly stating Japan's intent to attack Pearl Harbor, there were numerous red flags that should have alerted U.S. intelligence.

On October 9, 1941, a message was intercepted in which the Japanese counsel at Honolulu was assigned to provide a detailed report "on the types and number of American war craft at Pearl Harbor." For two weeks before the attack, code "Purple" was humming with hints of an impending assault. A message to the Japanese foreign minister in America instructed him to cease negotiations with the U.S. on November 29, after which "Things are going to automatically happen." On December 1, a message from Tokyo to Berlin alerted Hitler that hostilities between Japan and the U.S. were going to happen, "quicker than anyone dreams."

In spite of Marshall's warning, the base was unprepared. Planes were clustered on runways and ships in the harbor, making them easy targets. Antiaircraft guns were unmanned and, in fact, most of the military personnel were still asleep on a Sunday morning when the attack came.

HOW A SINGLE BOMB DELAYED THE END OF WORLD WAR II

In August 1944, German Field Marshal Günther "Hans" von Kluge realized the war was lost. He secretly contacted General George Patton, commander of the U.S. Third Army, and offered to surrender the entire Western Front to the Americans. Von Kluge was to get back in touch with Patton to arrange a meeting and discuss terms. Patton never heard back from him. A bomb from an Allied plane destroyed von Kluge's only radio truck.

Concerned that Adolf Hitler had learned of his contact with the Americans, von Kluge committed suicide, and the war continued for another nine months before Germany finally surrendered on May 7, 1945. Ironically, Hitler did not learn of von Kluge's plans until two weeks after the field marshal's suicide.

BEYOND THE CALL OF DUTY

In February 1951, U.S. troops in North Korea were fighting for survival from the bitter cold as well as hordes of Red Chinese. The fierce combat had taken a toll on platoon and squad leaders. That is how Corporal Einar Ingman found himself in command of two squads.

Leading his men against a machine-gun nest that was taking a deadly toll on his men, Ingman was struck in the side of his head by a grenade fragment that blew away his left ear. Still, he charged on, only to be struck in the face by a rifle bullet. Dazed, Ingman leaped into the machine-gun nest among the Chinese, slashing with his bayonet and firing his rifle. When there was no one left to fight, he staggered away and collapsed.

When Ingman's men reached the position, they were stunned to find that he had killed ten Chinese soldiers. Even more astonishing was the fact that Ingman survived his wounds to receive his Medal of Honor. Asked by a reporter why he did it, he replied: "That bullet through my head kind of made me quit thinking."

FACT OR FICTION?

LBJ LIED ABOUT THE GULF OF TONKIN INCIDENT

THE STORY: On the night of August 4, 1964, the three TV networks interrupted programming for a special report from the President. In somber tones, Lyndon Johnson announced that North Vietnamese gunboats had fired on U.S. ships in international waters in the Gulf of Tonkin on two separate occasions. He said that, even as he spoke, U.S. aircraft were on the way to bomb North Vietnam in reprisal. Johnson used the Gulf of Tonkin Incident to launch the nation into America's longest war—a conflict that would claim more than 58,000 American lives.

THE FACTS: On August 2, 1964, North Vietnamese PT-type gunboats did fire on the U.S. destroyer *Maddox.* However, the *Maddox* was not in international waters. It was within four miles of the North Vietnam coast supporting an attack by South Vietnamese gunboats on radar installations. CIA agents were on the gunboats with South Vietnam crews, directing the operation.

According to official reports, the *Maddox* fired on some enemy boats while they were still six miles away. That was well out of range for the North Vietnam boats. That would indicate the *Maddox* fired first.

Johnson claimed the North Vietnamese launched a second attack on the *Maddox* on the night of August 4. But Commander Jim Stockdale, a Navy fighter pilot responding to a distress call from the *Maddox,* flew over the area several times that night. According to Stockdale's report: "I found the destroyer sitting in the water firing at nothing."

There is no doubt that Johnson knew the circumstance of both alleged "attacks." Of the second incident Johnson blurted out in a briefing: "Hell! Those dumb sailors were just shooting at flying fish."

Why would Johnson lie to the American people? He was in a bitter Presidential campaign against Barry Goldwater, who was accusing him of being soft on communism. Johnson overcame the perception with the Gulf of Tonkin Incident and won the 1964 election. However, his escalation of the war and mismanagement of it forced him out of office in 1968.

CIVIL WAR SENTIMENTS
OF THE FIRST LADIES

SARAH POLK, widow of James K. Polk:

When the war began, she sold her slaves and declared her Tennessee farm to be neutral territory. Although she sympathized with the Confederacy, both sides respected her neutral declaration.

ANGELICA VAN BUREN, daughter-in-law of Martin van Buren:

A native of South Carolina living in the North, she sent blankets to Confederate prisoners housed at Elmira, N.Y.

JANE PIERCE, wife of Franklin Pierce:

An outspoken abolitionist, she advocated destruction of the South and confiscation of lands owned by slave holders.

ELIZA JOHNSON, wife of Andrew Johnson:

Although a native of Tennessee, she strongly supported the Union, prompting Confederate General E. Kirby Smith to evict her from her Tennessee home.

LUCY HAYES, future wife of Rutherford Hayes:

Worked as a volunteer nurse for the Union Army.

JULIA GARDINER TYLER, widow of John Tyler:

A New York debutante, her husband was serving in the Confederate legislature at Richmond when he died, leaving her his Virginia plantation. In spite of the Union blockade, she managed to ship a large quantity of cotton to the Bahamas, where it sold for high prices.

JULIA DENT GRANT, wife of Ulysses S. Grant:

She came from a slaveholding family and personally owned several slaves. During the war, she brought slaves with her when she visited her husband's camps.

Although Grant did not own slaves, he never asked his wife to give up her bondsmen.

MARY TODD LINCOLN, wife of Abraham Lincoln:

The spoiled daughter of a Kentucky slaveholding family, she was torn between her Southern family sympathies and her role as First Lady. Most of her family served in the Confederacy against her husband's Union armies.

ELLEN WILSON, future wife of Woodrow Wilson:

She came from a loyal Southern family. Wilson's second wife, Edith Galt Wilson, was accused of being a racist.

OTHERS:

Future First Ladies Lucretia Garfield, Caroline Harrison, Ida McKinley, Helen Taft, and Florence Harding all were members of pro-Union families.

WHY NEW YORK CITY CELEBRATED THE END OF WORLD WAR I FOUR DAYS BEFORE IT ENDED

On November 7, 1918, Admiral Henry Wilson, head of U.S. naval forces in France, received a telegram from Paris informing him that World War I was over. Wilson passed along the information to Roy Howard of United Press International, who promptly wired the good news to New York. The story hit the afternoon newspapers, and spontaneous celebrations broke out across the United States. However, no celebration equaled the one in New York City, which responded with a boisterous ticker-tape parade. The message received by Wilson was in error. The war did not end until November 11, four days after the New York celebration.

13 THINGS YOU MIGHT NOT KNOW
ABOUT THE PENTAGON

In the summer of 1941, as the U.S. geared up for a war that appeared inevitable, various War Department offices were located in seventeen buildings in Washington, D.C. The military brass convinced President Franklin Roosevelt that a single building was needed to centralize the department.

1. A team of architects was assigned to draw plans for the building in one weekend.
2. The original plan called for the building to be located at a site adjacent to Arlington Cemetery. Because of roadways and the configuration of that site, the architects designed the building in the shape of a pentagon.
3. There were objections from those who did not want to disturb the cemetery, prompting Roosevelt to select the present location for the building.
4. Ground was broken September 11, 1941. Thirteen thousand workers completed the job in just sixteen months in one of the most remarkable construction feats in the nation's history.
5. The cost was $83 million, twice the original estimate, and about the same as a battleship in 1941.
6. Roosevelt did not like the pentagon shape and wanted a more traditional building. However, the military brass liked it because the structure looked like a fortress. Since time was a factor, Roosevelt allowed construction to proceed.
7. Construction was so rapid that heavy earth-moving equipment, covered by fill dirt and concrete, remains entombed in the foundation.

8. The Pentagon was built in stages. As soon as each of its five sides was completed, it was occupied.

9. The Pentagon was built to accommodate up to 30,000 people and some 20,000 visitors a day. To handle the traffic, the first cloverleaf interchange was designed. The concept worked so well, the cloverleaf later was used in the interstate highway system.

10. The Pentagon has more than seventeen miles of hallways, 150 stairways, its own power plant, two hospitals, scores of cafeteria and dining rooms, and one elevator reserved for use by the Secretary of Defense.

11. A continuing complaint by the more than 25,000 workers is that it has only 284 restrooms, one for every 174 people who work there.

12. Roosevelt did not want windows in the building. He thought solid concrete walls would be stronger in the event of a bomb attack. Munitions experts convinced him that less damage would result if blowout windows were installed.

13. Roosevelt intended to convert the Pentagon to civilian use when the war ended.

MOCKING AMERICAN DEMOCRACY

When British troops occupied Washington, D.C., during the War of 1812, commanding officer Admiral Cockburn entered the Capitol building and called an assembly of his soldiers. "Gentlemen," he said, "the question is, shall this harbor of Yankee democracy be burned? All for it say aye!" As the chorus of ayes rose in the House chamber, Cockburn brought down the gavel. "Light up!" he said, and the Capitol was burned.

THE UNREAD MESSAGE
THAT CHANGED HISTORY

The winter of 1776 was a harsh one for George Washington's ragtag Continental Army. Driven out of New York and across New Jersey, his depleted ranks went into winter camp in the Pennsylvania wilderness. They were short on food and blankets. Some had rags bound around their feet because they did not have shoes. No one was more despondent than Washington, who confided to his staff: "Without a victory soon, I think the game might be pretty near up."

The best prospect for a quick victory to build the morale of his troops appeared to be at Trenton, New Jersey, where a garrison of Hessian troops was in winter quarters. It was decided the Continentals would cross the Delaware River and launch a surprise attack.

A spy in the Colonial area learned of the plan and crossed the river to warn the Hessian commander, Colonel Johann Rall. Upon reaching Trenton, the spy was told the colonel was busy. He penned a note detailing Washington's plans and gave it to an orderly.

As it turned out, the colonel was busy playing cards and drinking applejack. When an aide delivered the note to him, he slipped it in his jacket and forgot about it. On the morning of December 26, Rall awakened to the sounds of battle. Overnight, the Colonials had placed cannons on high ground overlooking Trenton. Supported by artillery, Washington's men swept through the town, routing the disorganized defenders and taking more than a thousand prisoners.

When it was over, Colonel Rall lay mortally wounded, the unread note still tucked in his pocket. Without the victory at Trenton, there is a possibility Washington's army might have disbanded before spring, ending the revolution.

THE STORM THAT STOPPED A WAR

In 1888, Emperor Otto von Bismarck wanted to establish a German colony in the Pacific and build port facilities for his ships. He dispatched a fleet of warships to occupy the Samoan Islands, ignoring American interests there.

The German ships shelled several islands, destroying the property of American citizens. In one incident, German troops landed and tore down an American flag. President Grover Cleveland responded by sending a fleet of warships to protect the Americans.

As the two fleets positioned for a looming battle, a massive hurricane swept across the region, sinking some of the ships and heavily damaging others. While captains fought to save their ships from the storm, American and German sailors found themselves being plucked from the ocean by the enemy.

Following the storm, the German ships returned home, and American Somoa became a protectorate of the United States. If the hurricane had not intervened, Germany and the U.S. almost certainly would have gone to war.

❦ NOTABLE QUOTE

"Our Army held the war in the hollow of their hand and they would not close it."

Lincoln, following the Battle of Gettysburg

FOOTNOTES TO HISTORY

* Upon learning of the death of George Washington, Napoleon ordered a mourning period of ten days throughout France.
* Among other facilities, the United States military operates 234 golf courses.
* The income tax is a legacy of the Civil War. President Abraham Lincoln signed it into law to pay for the war. The modern income tax was not approved until 1913.
* When Private Elvis Presley was stationed in Germany, he received up to 10,000 letters a week. His tag number was 53310761. His pay was $83.20 a month.
* General Douglas MacArthur's doting mother dressed him in skirts until he was seven years old. When he went to West Point, she accompanied him and rented an apartment that gave her a view of his dormitory room window.

THE PEARL HARBOR ALERT
THAT WAS IGNORED

SUNDAY, DECEMBER 7, 1941

7:00 a.m.—Radar operators Joseph Lockhard and George Elliott finished their shift at their station on the island of Oahu, Hawaii, but the truck that was to pick them up was late.

7:02 a.m.—Elliott was about to shut off his console when he picked up the largest blip he had ever seen. Thinking it was a malfunction, he asked Lockhard what he thought. Lockhard said they should report it to the control center.

7:05 a.m.—Elliott and Lockhard attempted to call the control center several times but got no answer. The men who were supposed to be on duty there had gone to breakfast.

7:15 a.m.—Elliott tried the regular phone circuit and got Lieutenant Kermit Tyler. Elliott told him: "Radar shows a large number of planes coming in from the north, three degrees east." Tyler said it probably was U.S. aircraft and told Elliott he should not worry about it.

7:20 a.m.—Lockhard called back and tried to convince Tyler that the situation appeared serious. "I have never seen this many planes on the screen," he said. Tyler told him there was nothing to worry about.

7:40 a.m.—The truck finally arrived to pick up Elliott and Lockhard.

7:45 a.m.—The operators shut down the station and left.

7:55 a.m.—Bombs began falling on Pearl Harbor.

A CUSSING BY GEORGE

By his nature, George Washington was calm and aloof, rarely letting his emotions show. But when riled, he was not above an occasional outburst of profanity. One observer who witnessed Washington dressing down General Charles Lee noted that he cursed Lee "'til the leaves shook on the trees." At the Battle of Kip's Bay, when Connecticut militia ran from the British without firing a shot, Washington went into a rage. According to witnesses, he threw his hat to the ground, began swinging his cane at anyone within reach, and cursed until he turned blue in the face.

GENERAL ECCENTRICITIES

* General Andrew Jackson thought the world was flat.
* Confederate General Richard Taylor could swear in Spanish, French, and English, which was the ethnic makeup of his Louisiana Tigers Brigade.
* Confederate General William Smith once rode into battle wearing a beaver stovepipe hat and waving a blue umbrella.
* General Zachary Taylor (father of Richard Taylor) never voted in an election—including the one that made him President.
* General Dwight Eisenhower hated cats. He ordered that any cat found on his property be shot.
* Confederate General Richard Ewell would sit in his tent and chirp like a bird. He also slept curled around the legs of a stool to relieve his back pain.

INDIANS AT BUNKER HILL

Although most Native American tribes sided with the British during the American Revolution, the Stockbridge Indians of western Massachusetts were loyal to the Colonial forces from the beginning of hostilities. Warriors from the tribe were in the ranks at the Battle of Bunker Hill.

"LITTLE BOY" WAS NOT SO LITTLE

The two atomic bombs dropped on Japan in 1945 each had an explosive impact equivalent to 20,000 tons of TNT. The bomb dropped on Hiroshima, named "Little Boy," was actually ten feet long and weighed 9,000 pounds.

THE BEST AND THE WORST CIVIL WAR GENERALS (according to the author)

THE 10 BEST UNION GENERALS

1. William T. Sherman
2. Ulysses S. Grant
3. George G. Meade
4. Winfield S. Hancock
5. Benjamin H. Grierson
6. Andrew J. Smith
7. James B. McPherson
8. George H. Thomas
9. John A. Logan
10. Andrew A. Humphreys

THE 10 WORST UNION GENERALS

1. John C. Fremont
2. Nathaniel P. Banks
3. Benjamin F. Butler
4. Ambrose E. Burnside
5. John Pope
6. Joseph Hooker
7. Egbert B. Brown
8. William B. Franklin
9. George B. McClellan
10. William S. Rosecrans

THE 10 BEST CONFEDERATE GENERALS

1. Thomas J. Jackson
2. Nathan B. Forrest
3. Robert E. Lee
4. James Longstreet
5. Patrick R. Cleburne
6. A. P. Hill
7. Richard Taylor
8. J.E.B. Stuart
9. William J. Hardee
10. Pierre Beauregard

THE 10 WORST CONFEDERATE GENERALS

1. Gideon Pillow
2. Braxton Bragg
3. John Pemberton
4. John B. Hood
5. David E. Twiggs
6. Theophilus Holmes
7. E. Kirby Smith
8. W.H.C. Whiting
9. William H. Carroll
10. Henry H. Sibley

ATTACK ON THE WHITE HOUSE

The only recorded incident of a militarylike attack on the White House took place February 17, 1974, when Private Robert Preston climbed into an Army helicopter at Fort Meade, Maryland, and headed for Washington, D.C. Alerted by military personnel, the Maryland State Police dispatched a helicopter to intercept him. The army chopper easily outraced the slower craft, setting off panic in the Executive Protection Service.

Arriving at the capital, Preston's helicopter hovered momentarily above the Washington Monument before heading directly toward the White House. It was met by a storm of small-arms fire that riddled the craft and brought it crashing to the lawn, a hundred feet from the White House. Private Preston, miraculously unhurt, was dragged from the smoking craft and hustled off to a mental hospital.

HOW A CIGAR WRAPPER DECIDED
THE OUTCOME OF A GREAT BATTLE

September 1862 was a critical time for the nation. Robert E. Lee's Army of Northern Virginia had defeated the Union Army in every major battle. Now Lee was taking the war to the north by invading Maryland. One great victory on northern soil not only would put Washington, D.C., under siege but likely bring recognition of the Confederacy by England and France.

That September an Indiana regiment took a break in a field where the Confederate Army had recently camped. As a soldier rested there, he spotted an envelope in the grass.

Opening it, he found three cigars wrapped in a piece of paper. While sharing the cigars with two buddies, he examined the paper. It appeared to be a set of orders for the Army of Northern Virginia.

The paper made its way up the ranks to the headquarters of Union General George McClellan, commander of the Union Army that stood between Lee and the nation's capital. McClellan quickly realized he was holding the marching orders for Lee's army. There in his hand was a guide to where Lee's army would be at any given time.

"Here is a paper with which if I cannot whip Bobby Lee I will be willing to go home," he told his aides.

Normally cautious, McClellan quickly organized a plan of attack. In the ensuing battle, he did not whip Lee but fought him to a draw at a little creek named Antietam. It was the bloodiest single day of the war—22,720 total casualties, with 3,650 killed. His army badly wounded, Lee retreated to Virginia.

A Confederate victory at Antietam might have changed the course of the war. That did not happen, because Bobby Lee lost his cigars.

☒ IT'S A FACT

---

* Early in World War II, as if U.S. military brass did not have enough to worry about, the army informed the media that it should not refer to American infantrymen as GIs, because it was short for "general issue," and that was demeaning to the men.
* During the Civil War, New England troops called their fellow soldiers from the Midwest "Gorillas," because of their rough language and rude behavior that often included looting.

THE BLOODY FINAL DAY OF WORLD WAR I

There were more casualties in the final six hours of World War I than there were on D-Day in World War II. The armistice to end the war was signed at five a.m. on November 11, 1918. It was to go into effect at 11 a.m. In those six hours, more than 11,000 casualties were recorded. Official records show that in those brief, closing moments of World War I, 320 Americans were killed and another 3,240 wounded.

A subsequent Congressional investigation described those figures as "conservative." French casualties were placed at 1,170 on the final day and the British at almost a thousand. The Germans suffered 4,120 killed, wounded, and missing. More than a thousand casualties were recorded by other armies.

Two factors contributed to the bloody toll: 1) French Field Marshal Ferdinand Foch and U.S. General John Pershing ordered Allied forces to continue attacking until the last minute; 2) Although the war was effectively over, several ambitious American generals ordered massive, last-minute attacks to secure territory and enhance their combat records.

Major General Charles P. Summerall sent elements of his V Corps across the Meuse River on a rickety pontoon bridge constructed overnight. The Marine 5th Infantry Regiment led the advance, stepping over the bodies of engineers who built the bridge, only to be virtually wiped out by artillery and machine-gun fire.

Major General William Wright sent regiments from the 89th Division to take the town of Stenay that morning.

Sixty-one were killed and 304 wounded in the attack. Wright later told a Congressional panel: "The men had been without bathing facilities for some time," thus placing cleanliness above human life.

◉ IT'S A FACT

* Marshal Foch did not want an armistice. He wanted to destroy the German Army. On November 7, the Germans sent a white-flag delegation to Foch's headquarters to surrender. The Frenchman refused to even see them.
* Foch delayed signing the armistice for almost forty-eight hours after terms of surrender were reached. Meanwhile, he ordered attacks to continue.
* In the U.S., complaints flooded Congress from the families of those killed or wounded on the final day of the war. No less than five Congressional investigations were conducted. No American general was ever reprimanded.
* The final casualty of the war was Private Henry Gunther. He was killed at 10:59 attacking a machine-gun nest even as the Germans tried to wave him back.

AN ICE-SKATING ARMY?

Following the Battle of Bunker Hill, Washington wanted desperately to attack the 10,000 British troops bottled up in Boston. One plan he drew up called for an advance force wearing ice skates to cross the frozen river at night and conduct a surprise attack. His staff talked him out of executing the plan. The British later withdrew and sailed to Nova Scotia.

THE GI BILL OF RIGHTS

On June 22, 1944, President Roosevelt signed into law the GI Bill of Rights, granting benefits to the veterans of World War II. Among the provisions:

1. Unemployment benefits of $20 a week for fifty-two weeks.
2. Guaranteed loans of up to $2,000 at not more than four percent interest to build homes or establish businesses.
3. Grants of $500 per year for education, plus payments of $50 to $75 per month for subsistence.
4. Up to $500 million for construction of new facilities for veterans.

FROM BATTLEFIELD TO CLASSROOM

Following the war, veterans flocked to the nation's college campuses under the GI Bill of Rights. By the fall semester of 1947, more than 1.25 million former soldiers were enrolled in colleges. The University of California alone reported more than 20,000 GIs in its classrooms. The result was the best-educated generation of Americans until that time, setting the stage for a period of U.S. growth and prosperity unmatched in history.

THE *MAYAGUEZ* INCIDENT

On May 12, 1975, Cambodian gunboats captured the U.S. registered merchantman *Mayaguez* and took its thirty-nine-man crew hostage. The following day, U.S. warships and 1,000 Marines descended on Koh Tang Island, where the *Mayaguez* was being held. Several Cambodian ships were sunk, but when Marines boarded the *Mayaguez,* the crew was missing.

Under threat of air strikes on the mainland, the Cambodian government finally released the crew. However, they missed the deadline for doing so. As a result, U.S. warplanes already in the air unleashed a thirty-minute bombardment of Cambodian military installations before the attack could be terminated. Fifteen U.S. Marines died in the assault on Koh Tang Island. The entire crew of the *Mayaguez* survived and was rescued.

D-DAY FACTS AND FIGURES

The greatest military invasion in the history of warfare took place December 6, 1944, when Allied forces assaulted the Normandy coast of France by sea, land, and air. The invading force consisted of:

* 38 convoys totaling 745 ships
* 4,066 landing craft
* 185,000 troops in the initial assault
* 18,000 paratroopers dropped behind enemy lines by 1,067 aircraft
* 20,000 vehicles plus 347 minesweepers landed in the first three days
* 13,175 combat aircraft to provide cover
* Within a month, 1,100,000 troops, 200,000 vehicles, and 840,000 tons of supplies were landed

---

◎ IT'S A FACT

In terms of manpower, the Allied invasion of Sicily on July 10, 1943, almost equaled that of D-Day. A force of 181,000 went ashore in less than three days.

THE STRANGE DEATH OF JAMES FORRESTAL

Well known is the tragic story of the aircraft carrier USS *Forrestal*. In 1967, while operating off the coast of North Vietnam, an accidental fire swept through the vessel, killing 134 crewmen. Little known is the tragic circumstance that plagued the man for whom the carrier was named.

James Forrestal was a navy veteran of World War I who became Secretary of the Navy in World War II. After the war he was appointed the first secretary of the newly created Defense Department and given the task of bringing all branches of the armed forces under one command structure.

Washington insiders considered Forrestal an organizational genius. Few realized that he suffered from what today might be diagnosed as chronic depression. In 1949, suffering from stress, Forrestal retired from the Defense Department. Two weeks later he checked into the U.S. Naval Hospital at Bethesda, Maryland.

On May 22, 1949, he placed a note on his bed, went to the window of his sixteenth-floor room, and jumped. His death shocked the nation. His doctors described his condition as "something like battle fatigue." The note included a line from Sophocles: "Comfortless, nameless, hopeless save in the dark prospect of the yawning grave."

THE BLOODIEST WAR

The bloodiest conflict in the history of warfare, by far, is World War II. Total deaths, including military and civilian, were placed at 54.8 million. Soviet Union fatalities alone are estimated at 25 million—most of them civilians. China suffered an estimated 7.8 million civilian deaths. The most devastated nation was Poland, which suffered 6,028,000 fatalities—22 percent of its population. According to official records, the United States military suffered 407,316 deaths in World War II.

LINCOLN AS A MILITIA CAPTAIN

During the Black Hawk Indian War, young Abe Lincoln was elected captain of his militia company. While drilling the men, he was marching them twenty abreast across a field when they came to a fence gate. "I could not for the life of me remember the command to get the company sideways so that it could get through the gate," he later recounted. He halted the men at the fence and dismissed them for a two-minute break, after which they were ordered to reassemble on the other side of the gate.

❧ NOTABLE QUOTES

* Included in George Washington's general orders of February 7, 1776: "Anyone attempting to retreat or desert will be instantly shot down."

WHAT REBEL GENERALS DID
AFTER THE CIVIL WAR

GENERAL RICHARD TAYLOR—Hired by international financier Samuel L. Barlow of New York, he was sent to England to handle Barlow's affairs. Taylor became a close friend of the Prince of Wales, soon to be King Edward VII. He awarded Taylor membership in the exclusive British Turf Club and sponsored him as an honorary member of the Marlborough Club, which was reserved for reigning princesses and their sons. Taylor returned to the U.S. in 1873 and died six years later at age fifty-three.

GENERAL EDMUND KIRBY SMITH—Fearing arrest, Smith sent a subordinate to surrender the Confederate Trans-Mississippi Department and fled to Mexico. There he lived very well with funds acquired by trading with the enemy during the war. Years later he returned to the United States and became president of the University of Nashville.

GENERAL JOE WHEELER—Wheeler eventually joined the United States Army and commanded troops in the Spanish–American War. He is remembered by historians for experiencing a Civil War flashback in the Battle of Las Guasimas in Cuba. In the heat of battle, he urged his U.S. troops forward, shouting: "Come on, boys! The Yankees are running! They are leaving their guns!"

GENERAL FITZHUGH LEE—The son of Robert E. Lee rose to the rank of major general in the U.S. Army and was commander of the VII Corps in the Spanish–American War.

GENERAL THOMAS JORDAN—He participated in the 1869 revolution in Cuba and rose to commander in chief of the rebel forces. The Cuban government put a $10,000 price on his head. When the revolution failed, Jordan escaped and returned to the United States.

CAMELS AND WAR ELEPHANTS IN AMERICA?

JEFF DAVIS AND THE CAMELS

When Jefferson Davis was U.S. Secretary of War in 1856, he purchased seventy camels for the U.S. Army. The camels were sent to an outpost in South Texas to provide transportation for soldiers in the rugged terrain. The camels proved their worth and were used successfully for two years before the experiment was abandoned.

ABE LINCOLN AND THE WAR ELEPHANTS

With the outbreak of the Civil War in 1861, Lincoln received an offer from the king of Siam to send him several dozen war elephants. Lincoln thanked the king and declined the offer.

✎ NOTABLE QUOTE

* Attorney General William Saxbe's reaction when a reporter informed him that President Nixon had authorized the bombing of Haiphong Harbor on Christmas Day: "He's out of his fucking mind!" Saxbe also referred to Nixon aides Ehrlichman and Haldeman as, "those two Nazis in the White House." Saxbe was appointed Attorney General by Nixon.

WHAT UNION GENERALS
DID AFTER THE WAR

Seven former Union generals became President of the United States. Others who did not reach such lofty heights include:

JOSHUA A. CHAMBERLAIN—A Medal of Honor winner for his heroics at Gettysburg, Chamberlain returned home to Maine a hero. He served four terms as governor and then became president of Bowdoin College. He died in 1914.

WILLIAM T. SHERMAN—Offered the Republican nomination for President, his reply became famous: "If nominated, I will not run; if elected, I will not serve." He became the highest-ranking officer in the U.S. Army before his retirement in 1884. He died in 1891 in New York City.

GEORGE MCCLELLAN—Bitter over losing the Presidential election to Lincoln in 1864, he moved to England. Asked why he moved, McClellan said he heard no slander about himself in England. After three years abroad, he returned to the United States and was elected governor of New Jersey.

AMBROSE BURNSIDE—Unsuccessful on the battlefield, he was very successful in business, earning a fortune in railroading after the war. Burnside also was a good politician, serving three terms as governor of Rhode Island and becoming a U.S. senator.

DAN SICKLES—He barely escaped court-martial after disobeying orders on the first day at the Battle at Gettysburg. The fact that he lost his leg generated sympathy and possibly saved him from the brig. After the war, Sickles became U.S. minister to Spain. A notorious womanizer, rumors circulated that he and Queen Isabella II had a torrid love affair. Years later he orchestrated a campaign for the Medal of Honor and received the award.

 IT'S A FACT

Sickles had the dubious distinction of making history in 1859 in a matter unrelated to his military service. He was a U.S. congressman when he shot and killed his wife's lover. His was the first known case in which a defendant was acquitted on a plea of temporary insanity.

12 STROKES FOR STEALING A MAJOR'S WIG

Sailors who complain of discipline in today's navy can be grateful they did not serve in the U.S. Navy in the 1840s. Listed here are actual punishments of U.S. sailors in 1848 for some unusual violations:

For stealing a major's wig	12 strokes
For bad cooking	12 strokes
Breaking into the liquor closet	12 strokes
Skulking	12 strokes
For running up debt on shore	12 strokes
For bad language	12 strokes
For being naked on deck	9 strokes
For throwing a spittoon overboard	6 strokes

A SIGNIFICANT ENCOUNTER

One of the first skirmishes of the Civil War took place at
Philipi, West Virginia, where a Union force under Major
General George McClellan routed a Confederate unit.
Wounded in the leg was a young rebel named James E.
Hanger.

The Union soldier who shot him was Ambrose Bierce,
destined to become one of the most popular writers of
Civil War stories in the last half of the nineteenth century.
But Hanger also gained fame. He was the first soldier of the
war to undergo a battlefield amputation. Hanger later built
his own artificial leg and, after the war, founded the J. E.
Hanger Company, which remains one of the largest man-
ufacturers of artificial limbs in the world.

In 1903, forty-two years after their meeting on the battlefield, Bierce visited Hanger. The writer announced that
he was the one who shot Hanger and dryly observed, "Well,
I see no new one has grown on." The remark cemented a
lasting friendship.

A TWIST TO THE STORY

In 1913, in his seventies and in poor health, Ambrose
Bierce simply disappeared, creating a mystery that still puz-
zles historians. He was last seen in El Paso, Texas, where he
stated his intention to join Pancho Villa's army in northern
Mexico. However, he earlier told friends and family that he
was going to the Grand Canyon, where he would commit
suicide "and nobody will find my bones." For almost a century researchers have sought the bones of Ambrose Bierce,
without success.

FIRST NONSTOP FLIGHT
AROUND THE WORLD

On March 2, 1949, an American B-50 bomber christened *Lucky Lady II* landed at Carswell Air Force Base, having completed the first nonstop flight around the world in ninety-four hours and one minute. The plane was refueled in air four times during the 23,452-mile flight. The reason for the flight? Air Force officials promptly announced that the United States now had the capability to drop an atomic bomb at any spot on earth at any time.

MEETING THE AGE REQUIREMENT
IN THE CIVIL WAR

Early in the Civil War, the first question a recruiter asked a volunteer was, "Are you over eighteen?" Some young men who wanted to join but did not meet the age requirement were conflicted at the prospect of telling a lie. They soon came up with a method to join up without lying. It was as simple as writing "18," on a piece of paper and placing it in one's shoe. When the recruiter asked if he was over eighteen, the volunteer could truthfully say, "Yes, sir!"

❧ NOTABLE QUOTE

★ When Harry Truman was informed that President Roosevelt was dead and he was the President, his reaction was: "Holy Jesus Christ and Andrew Jackson!"

TOKYO ROSE

In 1941, twenty-five-year old Iva Toguri, a U.S. citizen born in Los Angeles, boarded a plane to visit her aunt in Japan. She was trapped there following the Japanese raid on Pearl Harbor. Because she spoke perfect English, Iva was recruited by Tokyo Radio for propaganda purposes. Her radio program was broadcast throughout the South Pacific. Nicknamed Tokyo Rose, her soft, sultry patter and the American music she played made her popular among GIs stationed on remote islands. With the surrender of Japan, Iva was arrested in Yokohama and returned to the U.S. to stand trial for treason, of which she was convicted. In 1977, on President Gerald Ford's last day in office, he granted Iva a full Presidential pardon.

13 NATIONS THAT WAITED UNTIL 1945 TO DECLARE WAR ON GERMANY

Ecuador	Turkey	Saudi Arabia
Paraguay	Uruguay	Finland
Peru	Egypt	Argentina
Chile	Syria	
Venezuela	Lebanon	

THE ENEMY WHO BECAME OUR FRIEND

On June 12, 1944, the first German V-1 (Vengeance) rockets, launched from a base in the Baltics, fell on London, causing widespread panic. Within two weeks, the rockets had killed 2,752 Londoners. Just as Allied pilots were learning how to shoot down the V-1s, a more sophisticated V-2 version struck the city.

The mastermind behind the development of these weapons was Wernher von Braun. While still in his twenties, von Braun was considered Germany's top rocket scientist. His V-1 traveled at a speed of 370 miles per hour and delivered a ton of explosives. The V-2 was even faster and more accurate. If Adolf Hitler had allowed production earlier in the war, there is little doubt von Braun's rockets would have had a much greater impact on the outcome.

With the end of World War II, von Braun and his team of scientists were brought to the United States and went to work for the U.S. Army, developing weapons systems. Von Braun later was transferred to the U.S. civilian space program and led the development of the Saturn rockets that carried man to the moon.

WHY IT TOOK SO LONG
TO WHIP THE REBELS

When it appeared that England might recognize the Confederate government, Henry Ward Beecher, a preacher and firebrand abolitionist, traveled there for a series of speeches to rally support for the Union cause.

At Manchester, he found himself before a hostile crowd of rebel supporters who hooted and jeered each time he tried to make a point. Finally, an Englishman stood and wanted to know why the war had gone on for so long. "You said you would whip the Confederates in sixty days. Why haven't you?"

Exasperated, Beecher responded, "Because we found we had Americans to fight instead of Englishmen."

⬡ IT'S A FACT

Five Confederate generals and a commodore fought for the Imperial Mexican Army in the Juarista revolution. They were Mosby Parsons, Sterling Price, John Magruder, Joseph Shelby, and Commodore M. F. Maury. Parsons was killed in action. Several former rebel officers were hired to train the Egyptian Army.

THE 10 MOST CRITICAL BATTLES
IN U.S. HISTORY

By venturing a selection of the ten most critical battles in U.S. history, the author is aware of the skepticism such a list will generate. The operative word is "critical." These were encounters without alternative outcome. To have lost any of these battles might have altered American history:

Saratoga (1777)—Saratoga was not one but a series of battles fought over several weeks for control of the Hudson River Valley early in the Revolutionary War. The Colonial victory convinced France to back the Colonies with arms, supplies, and ships, without which the Revolution would not have succeeded.

Plattsburg (1814)—In a final effort to defeat the U.S. in the War of 1812, a British army of 11,000 invaded upstate New York. It was turned back at Plattsburg by an American force of 3,300 under General Alexander Macomb. With the loss, the Duke of Wellington told the British Parliament there was no way Great Britain could win the war, setting in motion peace talks that finally ended the conflict.

Buena Vista (1847)—After a series of spectacular victories in northern Mexico at the onset of the Mexican War, General Zachary Taylor came up against the elite core of Santa Anna's army, including 10,000 cavalry and more than 5,000 infantry, at Buena Vista. Though ill-supplied and outnumbered almost three to one, Taylor's troops virtually destroyed Santa Anna's army, effectively deciding the outcome of the war well before General Winfield Scott set out to capture Mexico City.

New Orleans (1862)—In the early-morning hours of April 24, 1862, Admiral David Farragut ran sixteen warships past the river forts protecting New Orleans and by midmorning the next day had captured the most vital city in the Confederacy. Some historians have called it the night the South lost the war. Not only did Farragut's bold action give the Union control of the lower Mississippi River, it deprived the rebels of the only city in the South with the wealth, population, and manufacturing base capable of sustaining a Confederate war effort.

Gettysburg (1863)—General Lee had an advantage at Gettysburg. He had options. Union General Meade had none. He had to defend Washington, D.C., at all costs. James Longstreet urged Lee to send the rebel army around the Union position at Gettysburg, find good defensive ground, and force Meade to attack him. Instead, Lee inexplicably sent his best troops in a virtual suicide charge into the concentrated strength of the Union Army at Cemetery Ridge. The resulting Union victory proved the turning point of the war.

Destruction of the Spanish Fleet (1898)—At daybreak on May 1, four cruisers and two gunboats under Admiral George Dewey steamed into Manila Bay in the Philippines and opened up on ten Spanish warships. In the ensuing battle, all ten Spanish ships were sunk. The American fleet did not lose a single vessel—or even a man. The result ensured a U.S. victory in the Spanish–American war and firmly established the United States as a global power.

Midway (1942)—On June 4, a Japanese fleet of ninety-eight warships, twenty-one submarines, and four aircraft carriers stood ready to take U.S.-held Midway Island in the Pacific. A U.S. fleet less than a third that size was all that stood between the Japanese and the California coast. The American force was losing the air battle when, in the span of a few minutes, U.S. dive bombers caught the Japanese carriers unprepared for an attack and sank three of them. When the fourth and final Japanese carrier was destroyed, the invasion fleet was left without air cover, forcing it to withdraw.

Guadalcanal (1942)—On August 7, U.S. Marines landed on Guadalcanal in the first U.S. attempt to take back an island occupied by the Japanese. The Marines clung to a small strip of the island and repelled repeated attacks by a superior Japanese force until reinforcements could be landed. Bitter fighting raged for six months before the U.S. finally drove the last of the Japanese from Guadalcanal and began an island-hopping campaign that would win the war in the Pacific.

D-Day (1944)—The greatest amphibious landing in history took place on the French coast at Normandy as the Allied armies began their campaign to take back Europe from the Germans. Fortunate for the Allies, the all-or-nothing gamble succeeded. If it had failed, the war might have gone on for years.

Inchon (1950)—With UN forces pinned down at the south tip of the Korean peninsula and their backs to the ocean, General Douglas MacArthur landed troops at the port city of Inchon, cutting off a large portion of the North Korean Army. UN forces then drove the North Koreans to the Manchurian border. Only the entry of China into the war prevented UN forces from destroying the North Korean Army.

HOW THE BATTLE OF BREED'S HILL BECAME THE BATTLE OF BUNKER HILL

We all know that the Battle of Bunker Hill actually was fought at Breed's Hill. Yet if one visits the site of the battle today, he will find that Breed's Hill has become Bunker Hill.

The confusion began in June 1775, when the Revolutionary Committee of Safety ordered Colonial officers to seize and fortify Bunker Hill against a possible attack by British troops occupying Boston. The officers responded by fortifying the wrong hill. Instead of Bunker Hill, they entrenched on Breed's Hill, some 2,000 feet away.

The battle took place there on June 17, 1775. For reasons unknown, it became popularly known as the Battle of Bunker Hill. Today, Breed's Hill, where the battle took place, is preserved as a historical site. It is called Bunker Hill. The original Bunker Hill is obscured by a residential development.

WHAT'S IN A NAME?

Civil War—Reb, Johnny Reb, Yank, Damnyank
Spanish–American War—Rough Rider
World War I—Doughboy
World War II—GI Joe, Swabby, Flyboy
Vietnam—Grunt

THE WIT OF GEORGE WASHINGTON

Historians have portrayed Washington as stern and aloof. Actually, he had a dry sense of humor that often endeared him to his troops.

* As Washington was preparing to cross the Delaware, his 300-pound artillery officer, Henry Knox, settled uneasily into the rocking boat. "Careful there, Hank," Washington cautioned. "You'll tip the boat and drown us all." The soldiers laughed, relieving the tension of the moment.
* At the first Constitutional Convention, a member proposed that the U.S. standing army be limited to no more than 5,000. Informed of the proposal, Washington said it was fine with him, if the members would add an amendment limiting any foreign invasion to only 3,000 troops.

TEDDY'S "BIG STICK" POLICY

When the Moroccan bandit Mulay Hamid El Raisuli demanded ransom for an American hostage named Ion Perdicaris in 1904, President Theodore Roosevelt sent a message to Moroccan rulers: "We want Perdicaris alive or Raisuli dead." He backed the demand by dispatching a fleet of warships to Morocco while announcing that he would speak softly but use the "big stick" when necessary.

Unknown to Roosevelt, a back-room deal between U.S. and Moroccan officials, involving a payment of $70,000 to Raisuli, had freed Perdicaris well before the fleet arrived. He also learned that Perdicaris was not an American citizen after all, having given up his U.S. passport in favor of Greek citizenship a year earlier. Still, Roosevelt did not call back the fleet for fear that he would lose face.

Although unnecessary, the mission convinced others that the United States stood ready to be a major player on the world stage.

THE FRIEND WHO BECAME OUR ENEMY

In 1945, a U.S. intelligence team parachuted into the jungles of Asia to assess the war in that region between communist guerrillas and the Japanese. The Americans were taken to the leader of the guerrillas and found him near death, suffering from malaria and dysentery. The team medic nursed him back to health.

The guerrilla leader, Nguyen Ai Quoc, was grateful to the Americans for saving his life. He offered to cooperate with the U.S. by providing intelligence and returning downed American pilots, a promise he kept.

The team urged military brass to provide arms and supplies to the guerrillas. The fact that Quoc was a communist required a decision by the White House. The request was still being considered when the war ended.

After the war, Quoc sought independence from French control for his country. He wrote to President Harry Truman, asking him to use his influence with the French to negotiate a peaceful solution. Truman refused to become involved. However, the United States would become involved. The guerrilla leader would become known by another name—Ho Chi Minh. His country was Vietnam.

WRONG HILL, TEDDY

There is a single image that tells the story of the Spanish–American War, and that is the one of Teddy Roosevelt and his Rough Riders charging up San Juan Hill at the Battle of Santiago in Cuba. But that is not precisely how it happened. There was a charge and there was a hill—but it was Kettle Hill, not San Juan.

When Roosevelt and his Rough Riders charged up Kettle Hill, they got to watch from the crest as the regular infantry routed the Spanish Army on nearby San Juan.

It was the press, not Roosevelt, who distorted the event. Roosevelt was candid when he noted in his memoirs that, from Kettle Hill, "We had a splendid view of the charge on the San Juan blockhouse."

By the time Teddy and his men reached San Juan Hill, the fighting was over.

AMERICA'S 2 MOST ACCLAIMED HEROES

SGT. ALVIN YORK

As a boy growing up in the Tennessee backwoods, York became a crack shot with a rifle in order to provide game for the dinner table. The skill served him well when he became a soldier in World War I and found himself alone, looking down a trench filled with German soldiers.

York began firing, cutting down one enemy rifleman after another. Ignoring return fire, he continued taking a deadly toll until the Germans began throwing down their weapons and raising their hands.

When it was over, twenty-eight lay dead in the trenches. Another 104 surrendered. Awarded the Medal of Honor, York returned to a ticker-tape parade in New York. Hollywood made a movie of his life in 1941. He died in 1964.

LT. AUDIE L. MURPHY

When Audie Murphy lied about his age to join the U.S. Army, there was nothing about the baby-faced seventeen-year-old to indicate that he would become the most deco-rated American soldier ever.

In combat in Europe, the young Texan demonstrated his heroism time after time and rose in rank from private to first lieutenant. But on January 26, 1945, outside Holtzwihr, France, he redefined the word "hero."

Facing an advance by a large German force, Murphy ordered his men to fall back. He then climbed atop a burning tank destroyer and used its machine gun to cover their retreat. Even as he raked the advancing Germans with machine-gun fire, he called in coordinates for an artillery barrage. Finally, as the enemy closed in and bullets whined around him, Murphy called for artillery on his own position. He leaped from the tank destroyer just before it exploded. Picking up a discarded rifle, he continued to cut down enemy soldiers until they started to retreat. Single-handed, he had turned back a major German assault.

In World War II, the U.S. awarded only five combat medals for heroism. Murphy won all five, including the Medal of Honor. Following the war, he became a movie actor, making several films, including *To Hell and Back,* the story of his life and wartime heroics.

VIETNAM TIMELINE

December 28, 1946—With the outbreak of fighting between French troops and Vietnamese rebels, Ho Chi Minh went into hiding and urged his people to arm themselves. "If you do not have a sword, arm yourselves with axes and clubs," he wrote. However, they had weapons—those left by the Japanese and Allies when they withdrew from Vietnam in World War II. What began as a guerrilla insurrection against French rule escalated into a bitter, twenty-five-year conflict that would entrap the United States in an unpopular war. Ironically, Ho was a U.S. ally in World War II.

February 7, 1950—The United States formally recognized South Vietnam as a separate nation.

June 1, 1950—President Truman authorized sending thirty-five military advisers to Vietnam to assist elements in the South opposing the communists.

July 20, 1954—Following defeat of the French Army at Dien Bien Phu by Viet Minh communists, a peace treaty was signed in Geneva. The country was officially divided into North and South Vietnam, and guerrilla warfare intensified in the South.

November 14, 1961—The number of U.S. military advisers in South Vietnam was increased to 900 with the dispatch of 200 Air Force instructors.

December 22, 1961—James Davis became the first American soldier "officially" killed in Vietnam when he and three Vietnamese regulars were ambushed near Saigon.

July 30, 1967—General William Westmoreland requested another 200,000 troops to supplement the 475,000 already serving in Vietnam.

January 27, 1973—A cease-fire by American forces in Vietnam went into effect after negotiators signed a truce agreement in Paris, France. The signing took place just five days after the death of Lyndon B. Johnson, who had escalated the conflict into a war that claimed 58,193 American lives.

HOW A PHOTOGRAPHER
TOOK 20,000 GERMAN POWS

In September 1944, Lieutenant Colonel Bertram Kalisch was a photographer and film producer for the U.S. Army Public Relations Department. He was stationed in Paris when he received a tip from a superior that "something significant" might be happening near Romorantin.

Gathering up cameras and a film crew, Kalisch sped south to the locale, where he found a bizarre situation. German Major General Erich Elster was sitting in the headquarters tent of a young American lieutenant named Magill. The lieutenant had convinced the general that the U.S. had far more troops in the area than was the case, and they were discussing a possible surrender of German forces in the area.

Once Elster learned that Kalisch was of German descent, the two got along well. Elster even invited the photographer to his headquarters, behind German lines. There, Kalisch finally convinced Elster that he should surrender. He promised to record a formal ceremony on film so there could be no doubt on the side of the Allies or Germans that it was an honorable surrender. Until that time, the largest number of German soldiers to surrender was 6,000, with the fall of Paris. Kalisch was stunned when he learned that Elster was surrendering 20,000 men.

THE 10 BEST AMERICAN GENERALS

(Selection based on field command performance)

THOMAS (STONEWALL) JACKSON (Civil War)—A meticulous planner, Jackson also had the ability to make rapid decisions when faced with the unexpected. His historic Valley Campaign alone qualifies him as one of the best military tacticians ever.

GEORGE S. PATTON (WW II)—He was the ultimate warrior. The only way to slow Patton was to withhold fuel for his tanks, which his superiors did. Otherwise he would have run across Europe and been in Berlin in a matter of weeks.

NATHAN B. FORREST (Civil War)—His strategy: "Get there first with the most." His hit-and-run tactics befuddled Union generals and prompted Sherman to label him, "that devil Forrest."

WILLIAM T. SHERMAN (Civil War)—He, indeed, believed war was hell and made it so for the South. A fearless battlefield commander, he was Grant's terrible swift sword. Sherman also was a master strategist when it came to planning a campaign.

DOUGLAS MACARTHUR (WW I, II)—His battlefield heroics in World War I earned him a Medal of Honor. His leadership in the Pacific in World War II and the landing at Inchon Harbor in the Korean War made him a legend. What MacArthur did not understand was the concept of limited warfare, which got him fired by a World War I artillery captain named Harry Truman.

ROBERT E. LEE (Civil War)—Not only was Lee a bold and masterful tactician, but no general since Napoleon had inspired such admiration from his troops. Outmanned and outgunned, he ended the careers of a succession of defeated Union generals before Grant overwhelmed his shrinking army with superior numbers.

OMAR BRADLEY (WW II)—He was known as the GI's general. But Bradley's secret to success was his ability to handle the egocentric generals under his command while directing American forces across Europe.

ULYSSES S. GRANT (Civil War)—"Unconditional Surrender" not only was a nickname, it was his approach to warfare. No general was better suited than Grant to fight a war of attrition. He would hang on the heels of a retreating army like a bulldog, which is how he finally whipped Bobby Lee.

ANDREW JACKSON (War of 1812)—Jackson's remarkable victory over the British at the Battle of New Orleans in 1815 qualifies him for any list of "best" generals. With a ragtag army composed largely of local militias, pirates, dockworkers, and citizen volunteers, he defeated a veteran British army that outnumbered him two to one, inflicting 2,100 casualties while suffering 71 in his own ranks.

ZACHARY TAYLOR (Mexican War)—With the outbreak of the Mexican War, Taylor commanded a small army sent to invade northern Mexico. Although badly outnumbered, he conducted a textbook campaign, winning victories at Palo Alto, Resaca de la Palma, and Monterey before virtually destroying the elite core of Santa Anna's army at Buena Vista.

❧ NOTABLE QUOTE

★ Commenting on the sorry performance of the short-range muskets issued to United States troops in the Mexican War, U.S. Grant noted: "A man might fire at you all day without your finding it out."

THE 10 WORST AMERICAN GENERALS

JAMES WILKINSON (War of 1812)—Sent to invade Canada with 4,000 men, Wilkinson was turned back by 200 British regulars.

HORATIO GATES (American Revolution)—During the critical Battle of Bemis Heights at Saratoga, Gates sat in his tent discussing politics with a captured Englishman while Benedict Arnold slugged it out with John Burgoyne's British Army. Gates then took credit for the victory.

GIDEON PILLOW (Civil War)—When Grant closed in on Fort Donaldson, Pillow ordered his subordinate to surrender, then fled the scene. His cowardly action allowed Grant to capture 15,000 rebel troops, large quantities of arms and supplies, and most of Tennessee. Pillow was so incompetent that in the Mexican War he became disoriented and had his men entrench with their backs to the enemy.

WILLIAM H. WINDER (War of 1812)—Commander of the army protecting Washington, D.C., Winder's troops were so ill-organized they were routed in one charge by an outnumbered British force. At the Battle of Stoney Creek, Winder was defeated although his troops outnumbered the British three to one.

WILLIAM WRIGHT (World War I)—With less than six hours until the armistice, Major-General Wright sent several regiments from the 89th Division to take the town of Stenay for no good reason but to enhance his resumé. He captured the heavily fortified town at a cost of 61 soldiers killed and another 304 wounded. His excuse when called before Congressional investigators:

"The men had been without bathing facilities for some time."

AMBROSE BURNSIDE (Civil War)—The Stone Bridge debacle at Antietam Creek; the notorious "Mud March"; the "Battle of the Crater";—it was no coincidence that, if there was a Union disaster in the making, Burnside was there.

BRAXTON BRAGG (Civil War)—Bragg had one strategy: Find the strength of the enemy position and attack it. It was a strategy that contributed to the destruction of two rebel armies—the Army of the Mississippi and the Army of Tennessee. His irrational decisions at Missionary Ridge, mercifully for his abused troops, finally got him removed from command.

JOHN C. FREMONT (Civil War)—More politician than warrior, Fremont was repeatedly embarrassed by Stonewall Jackson. The ultimate humiliation took place at Port Republic, where Union armies under Fremont and General James Shields had Jackson trapped between them and he whipped both.

WILLIAM TRAVIS (Texas Independence)—Although technically not an American general, the hero of the Alamo deserves a spot in our top ten simply for taking on a 6,000-man Mexican army with 182 volunteers. Still, instead of concentrating his meager forces, Travis had them widely dispersed, trying to defend a large compound around the Alamo. It mattered little, since Santa Anna's army would have overrun the position under any circumstance.

E. KIRBY SMITH (Civil War)—The commander of Confederate forces west of the Mississippi River, Smith was more interested in clandestine cotton trading with Northern speculators than military matters. His ill-advised plan to retake Little Rock and St. Louis in the spring of 1864 resulted in an ignoble defeat by an inferior Union force at Jenkins' Ferry, Arkansas.

THE WORST GENERAL
IN AMERICAN HISTORY

Without peer, James E. Wilkinson was the worst general ever to wear a U.S. uniform. Not only was he a gross incompetent, militarily speaking, he was corrupt beyond redemption. President James Madison ordered him to be court-martialed in 1811, but he was found not guilty.

At the outbreak of the War of 1812, Wilkinson was the highest-ranking officer in the U.S. Army. He also was a con man and thief who manipulated army supply contracts and pocketed huge sums in the form of kickbacks. He was a land speculator who duped investors. During the American Revolution he conspired with Thomas Conway and Horatio Gates in an unsuccessful attempt to get George Washington fired. He conspired with Aaron Burr to seize New Orleans and establish a separate nation west of the Mississippi River. He then betrayed Burr.

Wilkinson conspired with the governor of Louisiana to jail his political enemies, then turned on the governor. He became a spy for the Spanish government, receiving $2,000 a year until he betrayed Spain.

In spite of all of this, Wilkinson is best remembered for suffering perhaps the most ignoble military defeat in U.S. history, worse even than Custer's debacle at Little Big Horn. In 1814, leading an army of 4,000 at Lacolle Mills, Canada, Wilkinson was turned back by a force of 200 British regulars.

IKE'S MOM

Dwight Eisenhower's mother was a stern disciplinarian. She also was a pacifist. When she caught young Ike reading some books about war, she confiscated them and forbade him to read such material in the future.

THE AMERICAN WHO FREED CONVICTED NAZI WAR CRIMINALS

In 1951, an American bureaucrat signed an order freeing twenty-eight convicted Nazi war criminals. He then reduced the sentences of an additional sixty-four German prisoners convicted of war crimes and postponed the execution of ten others.

With his pen, John J. McCloy undermined the sentences handed down in the post World War II Nuremberg Trials.

McCloy was High Commissioner of the U.S. Zone in occupied Germany when he began granting mass clemency to German prisoners even as wanted Nazi criminals were still being hunted around the world. McCloy weathered a storm of criticism. His reaction was that he was simply applying American judicial law to the cases. Others saw a more sinister motive behind the releases. They saw it as a means to release arms manufacturer and convicted war criminal Alfred Krupp without generating suspicion of favoritism.

What is known is that on February 1, 1951, Krupp and his eight-member board of directors walked out of Landsberg Prison free men.

TWO UNLIKELY CONTRIBUTORS
TO THE AMERICAN MILITARY

THE CONVICT WHO INVENTED
THE CARBINE RIFLE

The semiautomatic M1 carbine was the favorite weapon of the American GI in World War II. General Douglas MacArthur called it "one of the strongest contributing factors to our victory in the Pacific." Even more fascinating than the weapon is the story of the man who invented it.

David Marshall Williams was a North Carolina moonshiner. When lawmen raided a still in 1921, an exchange of gunfire resulted in the death of a deputy sheriff. Although Williams swore that he never fired a shot, he was convicted of murder. There was just enough doubt that, instead of the death penalty, he was given a thirty-year sentence.

Although Williams was a man of limited education, the prison warden quickly realized that he was a mechanical genius. Given free rein by the warden, Williams designed and built several innovative guns in prison. Called on the carpet by his superiors, the warden said he trusted Williams to the extent that if the convict ever used one of his guns to escape, he (the warden) would serve out his sentence.

Among the weapons he built was a lightweight handheld machine gun. It featured a short-stroke piston that used the explosive force of firing one bullet to load the next one.

Paroled after eight years in prison, Williams was hired by the Winchester Company. In 1941, the U.S. Army sponsored a competition to produce a light semiautomatic rifle.

Williams won, and the army named his weapon the M1 Carbine. More than six million of them were produced during World War II.

Williams eventually held more than sixty patents. There is hardly an automatic weapon today that does not include one of his ideas.

THE MOVIE STAR WHO INVENTED FREQUENCY-HOPPING

Her real name was Hedwig Kiesler. She was breathtakingly beautiful and by the time she was a teenager had become a movie star in Europe. She married a wealthy Austrian arms dealer named Fritz Mandl. He was a Nazi sympathizer who kept his teenage bride a virtual prisoner. She escaped by climbing out a two-story window, fleeing across Europe and eventually to the United States and Hollywood.

Changing her name, Hedwig became a screen sensation and was billed as the "most beautiful woman in the world." But she also had brains. She had heard her husband talk about the jamming of signals emitted from radio-controlled torpedoes. In 1942, a solution to the problem came to her while she was dining. On the back of a cocktail napkin, she sketched out the concept of frequency-hopping to prevent signal-jamming.

A friend, composer George Antheil, was so impressed he convinced her to patent the idea. It turned out to be a revolutionary new concept, far ahead of its time. Although the U.S. military was interested, it did not develop the system until well after World War II. Its first effective military use was during the Cuban Missile Crisis.

Today, her system is known as spread spectrum technology. It is an important part of cell phone and satellite communications, and it is used in munitions guidance systems.

The inventor was actress Hedy Lamar. Because her patent had expired before it was used, she never received a dime for it.

THE DUEL THAT ANDREW JACKSON LOST

During the War of 1812, Thomas Hart Benton was one of Andrew Jackson's most trusted aides, but after the war the two got into a quarrel over an obscure point of honor. Because of Jackson's reputation as a duelist, Benton avoided him until one day in Nashville when he and his brother were crossing a street and spotted Jackson coming toward them with pistol in hand. Both of the brothers fired their pistols, and a bullet struck Jackson, wounding him.

Afraid Jackson would seek revenge, the Benton brothers fled to Missouri. Years later, Benton had become an influential senator from Missouri when Jackson arrived in Washington. There was speculation that Old Hickory would shoot him on sight. Instead, the two made peace.

When Jackson was elected President, Benton became one of his most trusted advisers. Some twenty years after the shoot-out at Nashville, Jackson had the bullet removed from his body. When he saw Benton, he held out the bullet and said, "Here, I think this belongs to you." Benton declined the offer, noting that, since Jackson had carried it around for twenty years, it rightfully belonged to him.

MONUMENT TO A TRAITOR

Near Saratoga Springs, New York, sits the only known monument to a traitor. No name appears on the granite memorial, just a relief showing a cannon, the epaulet of a major general, a wreath, and a military boot for the left leg. It is titled, simply, the "Boot Monument." Oddly, it is a tribute to Benedict Arnold, the man who betrayed his country.

Before his name became synonymous with the word "traitor," Arnold was a hero of the American Revolution. Most military historians agree that he probably was the Continental Army's best battlefield general.

At Saratoga, Arnold led the Colonials to a series of brilliant victories against an 8,000-man British Army under General John Burgoyne. He then circled behind the British, cut off their retreat, and forced Burgoyne to surrender his entire army. If Burgoyne had prevailed at Saratoga, the Hudson River Valley would have fallen into British hands, cutting the colonies in two. For all practical purposes, the American Revolution would have been over. Instead, Saratoga inspired the French to enter the conflict, providing critical arms and supplies to the Continental Army.

Sorely mistreated by Congress, Arnold was denied promotions he had earned, and he saw others receive credit for victories he won. When he was assigned command of the fort at West Point, effectively confining him to desk duty, it was the final straw. He went over to the side of the British.

The monument to the nameless hero at Saratoga is a tribute to Arnold's victory there. The left boot in the relief leaves no doubt. Arnold was wounded in the left leg at Saratoga.

MILITARY ORIGIN OF
COMMON WORDS AND PHRASES

STONEWALL—In the first major battle of the Civil War at Bull Run Creek, a Union assault threatened to break the rebel line at Henry Hill. However, late-arriving Virginia troops under General Thomas Jackson plugged the breach and refused to yield. As the battle raged, General Bernard Bee shouted to his disorganized Texas troops: "Look! There stands Jackson like a stone wall! Rally behind the Virginians!" Within minutes, the man who immortalized Jackson as "Stonewall" lay dead on the field. In contemporary language, if one "stonewalls" an issue he stands firm and refuses to yield. A more sinister definition applies to government attempts to cover up detrimental information.

PIPE DOWN—In the era of sailing vessels, the noise of wind and waves often made it difficult for sailors to hear orders by their officers. The problem was solved by a special pipe used by the boatswain. It emitted high-pitched notes that could be heard over a storm. One signal was to "pipe the men down," or send them below deck. At the U.S. Naval Academy the term was modified. "Pipe down" called for silence in the ranks.

SIDEBURNS—When General Ambrose Burnside was given command of the Army of the Potomac, he sported a unique facial hairstyle. Instead of the traditional beard, he shaved his chin, leaving only a mustache and a heavy growth of hair in front of his ears. The style quickly caught on and the men soon were wearing "burnsides." Notoriously inept, Burnside's role as commander of

Union forces was brief, but his name lives on even though the syllables have become reversed.

BLOCKBUSTER—During World War II, a high-explosive bomb was developed. Capable of leveling a city block, it was called a blockbuster. Hollywood quickly borrowed the word to describe a movie sure to have a big impact on audiences.

NAVAL POWER ON THE EVE OF WORLD WAR I

As of July 1, 1913, *Nauticus,* the German yearbook on naval forces, listed the strength of various navies. Judging from the number of war vessels under construction, it was obvious that the United States, as well as the European nations, was preparing for World War I well before hostilities began. The numbers below represent active vessels with those under construction in parentheses. Germany classified the number of submarines it had under construction:

COUNTRY	ARMORED CRUISERS	WARSHIPS	SUBMARINES
Great Britain	42 (2)	27 (11)	70 (25)
Germany	13 (3)	15 (11)	23 (NA)
France	22 (0)	8 (10)	60 (15)
United States	15 (0)	8 (6)	30 (20)
Japan	14 (3)	5 (7)	13 (2)
Russia	6 (4)	0 (11)	30 (25)
Italy	10 (0)	1 (8)	20 (4)
Austria– Hungary	3 (0)	2 (3)	6 (2)

A REACTION TO CUSTER'S LAST STAND

"I regard Custer's massacre as a sacrifice of good troops, brought on by Custer himself, that was unnecessary—wholly unnecessary."

President Ulysses Grant

SHEEP ON THE WHITE HOUSE LAWN

At the beginning of World War I, as a symbolic gesture, President Wilson purchased a flock of sheep to replace the White House gardeners who were drafted into the war. The sheep did a good job of keeping the lawn trimmed, but First Lady Edith Wilson wanted to do something more for the war effort. She arranged to sell the wool from the flock and donate the funds to the Red Cross. By the end of the war, Edith and her sheep raised $100,000 for the Red Cross.

INCREDIBLE FEATS BY U.S. AIRMEN

U.S. military technology apparently was far ahead of its public-relations skills in the early years of flight. While pilots like Charles Lindbergh and Wiley Post were being hailed as heroes, unsung U.S. Army and Navy fliers were setting records:

LT. COMMANDER ALBERT (PUTTY) READ

It was Read, not Lindbergh, who flew the first aircraft across the Atlantic Ocean. Lindbergh was only seventeen years old when Read made the flight in 1919. Lindbergh did not accomplish the feat until 1927. Read and a five-man crew took off from Newfoundland, Canada, in a Curtiss NC-4 flying boat they christened the "Lame Duck" and flew to the Azores. From there they went to Lisbon, Portugal, and finally to England, covering 4,717 miles.

FOUR U.S. ARMY PILOTS

An incredible aeronautic feat that took place in 1924 has been virtually forgotten by history. Four U.S. Army fliers circled the earth in two Army Douglas DWC amphibian aircraft. Lt. Lowell H. Smith and Lt. Leslie P. Arnold piloted one of the planes, Lt. Erik H. Nelson and Lt. John Harding the other. The dual-wing planes took off from Seattle, Washington, and landed back there after 26,345 miles. The planes were named the *Chicago* and *New Orleans*.

MAJOR CLYDE PANGBORN AND HUGH HERNDON

The first nonstop flight across the Pacific Ocean was accomplished by Pangborn and Herndon in a Bellanca cabin aircraft they named *Miss Veedol*. They took off from Sabishiro, Japan, on October 4, 1931, and landed at Wenatchee, Washington, forty-one hours and 4,558 miles later.

★ IT'S A FACT

★ Lindbergh also was not the first to fly nonstop across the Atlantic. That was accomplished by two Canadian fliers in a Vickers bomber in 1919. Lindbergh's claim to fame—he was the first to fly alone across the Atlantic.

A CHRONOLOGY OF AMERICA'S
FOREIGN MILITARY INVOLVEMENT

1775–1781 The American War for Independence. Continental forces invaded Canada, putting Quebec City and Montreal under siege. In 1777, John Paul Jones, commanding the warship *Ranger,* took the war to the shores of Great Britain, invading English ports and harassing shipping. Colonial Navy captured Nassau in the Bahamas from the British.

1801 Thomas Jefferson sent a U.S. Navy fleet to the Mediterranean to fight the Barbary pirates who were holding American merchant ships and seamen hostage.

1805 A second U.S. fleet was dispatched to Tripoli. Marines captured the fortress of Derna and hoisted the American flag on foreign soil for the first time.

1806 Captain Z. M. Pike invaded Spanish–held Mexico at the headwaters of the Rio Grande.

1812 With the beginning of the War of 1812, the first of several unsuccessful invasions of Canada took place. President Madison and Congress authorized the invasion and occupation of Spanish-held Amelia Island off the coast of Florida.

1813 General James Wilkinson seized Mobile Bay from the Spanish. In another action, U.S. forces seized Nuka Hiva in the Marquesas Islands to protect American ships from the British.

1814 Andrew Jackson invaded Spanish territory to capture Pensacola and drive out British troops using it as a sanctuary.

1815 A U.S. fleet, backed by warships from several European countries, soundly defeated the Barbary pirates, ending harassment of American ships in the Mediterranean.

1816 U.S. forces invaded Spanish Florida and destroyed Nicholls Fort. Andrew Jackson was dispatched to subdue the Seminole Indians in Florida.

1817 President Madison sent a U.S. fleet to expel bandits and smugglers, who were raiding towns in U.S. territory, from Spanish-held Amelia Island.

1818 Spain was forced to sell Florida to the U.S. for $5 million. Jackson completed the Seminole War by driving the few surviving natives deep into the swamps.

1822 A U.S. force invaded Cuba in pursuit of pirates. In the next three years several additional landings took place in Cuba.

1824 Commodore David Porter, with 200 men, captured the town of Fajardo in Spanish-held Puerto Rico, which was sheltering pirates. When Spain complained, Porter was made a scapegoat and court-martialed.

1825 U.S. Marines invaded Cuba twice to capture pirates harassing American merchantmen.

1827 Marines aboard the USS *Warren* were sent to the Mediterranean to flush pirates from Greek islands of Argenteire, Miconi, and Androse.

1831 When bandits on the Falkland Islands (Argentina) seized three American sealing ships, the USS *Lexington* arrived to bombard a settlement on the island and free the crews.

1832 A U.S. naval force stormed Sumatra to punish the natives for plundering an American ship and killing its crew. The town of Quallah Battoo was leveled and 150 islanders killed. Two U.S. soldiers were killed.

1833 U.S. soldiers occupied Buenos Aires, Argentina, to protect American business interests there during an insurrection.

1835 Marines were sent to Callao and Lima, Peru, to protect American interests during an attempted revolution.

1836 Another revolution erupted in Peru, and the Marines were sent back to suppress it.

1838 A U.S. force returned to Sumatra to punish natives for killing the crew of another American merchantman and plundering its cargo. The town of Muckie was burned.

1840 An expedition force invaded the Fiji Islands after natives attacked American exploration and scientific teams. Several villages were set ablaze.

1841 A second U.S. force landed on Samoa after natives murdered an American seaman.

1843 Four U.S. warships and 200 Marines landed on the Ivory Coast of Africa to punish natives for attacks on American seamen. In Canton, China, Marines from the USS *St. Louis* restored order after fights broke out between Americans and Chinese.

1844 Marines returned to Canton to crush a series of Chinese riots against foreigners.

1849 A U.S. naval fleet steamed into the Ottoman city of Smyrna to force the release of an American who had been seized by the Austrians.

1851 The USS *Dale* attacked Johanns Island on the east coast of Africa after local officials arrested the captain of an American whaling ship.

1852 U.S. forces were dispatched to Argentina to protect American interests during a revolution.

1853 Marines returned to Argentina in April. Meanwhile, a U.S. force was sent to Nicaragua in a period of political upheaval. Commodore Matthew Perry's fleet arrived at Tokyo Bay with a show of force that convinced Japan to agree to Western trade after more than 200 years of isolation.

1854 U.S. Navy bombarded San Juan del Norte, Nicaragua, after a mob attacked the American minister. American and British warships landed troops in Shanghai to protect business interests during a civil uprising.

1855 A combination of U.S. and European forces landed at Montevideo, Uruguay, to protect business interests during a revolution. A U.S. fleet engaged in a fight with pirates near Hong Kong. The Navy landed on Fiji Island to extract reparations for the murder of American citizens.

1856 Marines landed in the Republic of New Granada (Panama) to protect the Atlantic–Pacific Railroad during political unrest. It was the first of five interventions there. With the outbreak of the Opium War between China and Great Britain, Marines landed at Canton and fought a pitched battle, killing 500 Chinese. Seven Marines were killed.

1857 The Navy and Marines arrived in Nicaragua to arrest William Walker, a U.S. citizen who had led a filibuster revolution and established himself as president.

1858 Two warships with Marines were sent to Uruguay to protect U.S. citizens in another revolution. The Navy returned to Fiji to punish natives for murdering Americans. Several warships were dispatched to Ottoman, Turkey, to display U.S. force after several Americans were massacred at Jaffa.

1859 A U.S. force was sent to Shanghai to protect Americans when the second Opium War broke out.

1860 U.S. troops landed in Colombia to protect American business interests. U.S. and British forces invaded

Angola, Africa, to protect American and English citizens and their property.

1861–1865 The American Civil War claims 503,324 American lives in the North and South, according to official records. However, most historians place the number at more than 650,000.

1863 The USS *Wyoming* attacked Shimonoseki, Japan, in retaliation for an assault on the American ship *Pembroke*.

1864 Marines were dispatched to protect the U.S. trade minister to Japan.

1867 Marines returned to Nicaragua in a period of political unrest. A naval force landed on Formosa (now Taiwan) and burned villages after natives killed the crew of a wrecked American vessel.

1868 A large U.S. force invaded Japan and took control of five major cities to protect American interests during a civil war that led to the Meiji Restoration.

1871 U.S. soldiers captured and destroyed five Korean forts in retaliation for the murder of the crew of the American ship *General Sherman*. In the fighting, 243 Koreans and four Americans were killed.

1885 The USS *Wachusett* was sent to Guatemala to protect American lives and property. For the first time, the term "Gunboat Diplomacy" appeared in U.S. newspapers.

1891 U.S. gunboats were sent to the Bering Strait to stop seal poaching by the Russians.

1893 When wealthy American sugar-plantation owners staged a coup against Hawaii's ruling queen, Marines were sent to protect American lives and property. President Grover Cleveland condemned efforts to annex Hawaii, but his successor, William McKinley, did so in 1898.

1895 Marines stationed in China fought at Peking and Newchwang to protect American nationals.

1898 The Spanish–American War was triggered by a mysterious explosion on the USS *Maine* in Havana Harbor that killed 266 sailors. U.S. troops defeated Spanish forces in Cuba, and the Navy destroyed the Spanish fleet in the Pacific. The fighting extended to the Philippines. The war lasted 178 days, during which time 2,983 Americans died. The U.S. gained control of Cuba, the Philippines, Guam, and Puerto Rico as a result of the conflict.

1899 U.S. forces were sent to protect American interests in Nicaragua during a local military attempt to take over the government. Spain ceded the Philippines to the U.S. for $20 million. A rebellion by the Filipinos resulted in a three-year guerrilla war in which 4,324 Americans were killed and 2,840 wounded. More than 16,000 Filipino combatants were killed.

1900 Marines were sent to Peking to protect Americans during the Boxer Rebellion. Fifty-three Marines were killed in the action, 235 wounded.

1901 U.S. forces were sent to protect rail lines across the Panama isthmus during a local revolution.

1902 U.S. used warships and Marines to seize the Panama isthmus from Colombia.

1904 President Theodore Roosevelt sent a large fleet to Tangier, Morocco, to free an American being held for ransom. It turned out that the "American" was actually a Greek citizen.

1905 Troops were sent to Honduras to protect Americans during political unrest.

1906 U.S. forces landed in Cuba to restore order following an insurrection. The troops remained there for three years until a stable government was established.

1907 When Honduras and Nicaragua went to war, U.S. soldiers were dispatched to protect citizens and American interests.

1910 Troops landed in Nicaragua, ousted President Zelaya and installed Adolfo Diaz, who was more friendly to U.S. business interests.

1911 Troops were dispatched to Honduras to restore President Manuel Bonilla to power after he was overthrown by liberal-leaning insurgents. Marines landed at Shanghai, China, to protect U.S. citizens as riots signaled the beginning of a nationalistic revolution.

1912 U.S. forces were dispatched to Nicaragua to prop up the Diaz government, threatened by revolution. U.S. troops would remain there for the next twenty-two years.

1914 During a revolution in the Dominican Republic, the U.S. Navy used gunfire to stop the bombardment of Puerto Plata by rebel factions.

1914–1917 A state of undeclared war with Mexico existed for three years, triggered by Pancho Villa's raids into the U.S. and the Dolphin Affair, in which Mexican soldiers detained and harassed American sailors. U.S. forces made several incursions into Mexico. On one occasion, General Pershing pursued Villa 400 miles into Mexico, and U.S. Marines occupied Vera Cruz for six months.

1915–1934 American troops were stationed in Haiti during a period of almost continuous unrest. Haiti became a U.S. protectorate under an agreement between the two countries.

1916–1924 Marines were stationed in the Dominican Republic following twenty-eight revolutions in fifty years. By the time U.S. forces were withdrawn in 1924, 144 Marines had been killed in action.

1917–1918 The U.S. entered World War I with a declaration of war against Germany on April 6, 1917. In the next eighteen months, the U.S. would suffer casualties of 116,708 killed and 204,002 wounded. Meanwhile, an American force was sent to Cuba to stop an insurrection. American forces remained there for three years. Troops invaded Mexico three times in 1918 to pursue bandits raiding border towns. In the summer of 1918, U.S. ships blockaded Russian ports and 7,000 U.S. troops landed at Vladivostok in Eastern Russia to assist counterrevolution forces against the Communist Red Army. Another 5,000 troops were sent to Archangel. All troops were withdrawn from Russia by 1920.

1920 Troops landed in Guatemala to protect U.S. officials and citizens during an insurrection. Marines were sent back to a Russian island in the bay of Vladivostok to protect American interests. They remained there for two years.

1922 U.S. forces in Guatemala were instrumental in overthrowing President Carlos Herrera for a government more friendly to Sam Zemurray's United Fruit Company.

1926 Marines were sent back to Nicaragua to protect American citizens and property. The Soviets were accused of trying to foment communist revolutions in Nicaragua and Mexico. In fighting over several years, 133 Marines were killed.

1927 Marines used warplanes in Nicaragua to disperse insurgents surrounding U.S. troops at Ocotal, killing more than 300. Reinforcements were sent to China in the wake of a nationalist uprising. U.S. warships bombarded Nanking to protect the American consulate.

1933 U.S. warships were sent to Cuba as a show of force in support of Fulgencio Batista, who had emerged as president following a revolution. Significantly, President Franklin Roosevelt refused to send in U.S. troops, declaring he wanted to "break the habit" of armed intervention.

1937 The U.S. supported Anastasio Somoza in his successful attempt to overthrow the government of Nicaragua.

1941 Well before entering World War II, U.S. warships were battling German submarines in the Atlantic.

1941–1945 The U.S. entered World War II. From Pearl Harbor to Nagasaki, more than 400,000 Americans were killed. With the end of the war, U.S. forces were stationed in locales around the globe to counter the threat of communism spreading beyond the Soviet Union.

1946 Korea was divided. American forces occupied South Korea and established direct military rule until 1948.

1948 Marines were sent to Nanking, China, to protect the American embassy as the city fell to the communists. Troops landed at Shanghai to evacuate American citizens as another communist takeover loomed.

1950 Caught unprepared, U.S. regulars and reserves were rushed to South Korea after a massive North Korean Army poured across the 38th Parallel in a surprise attack. The war would continue for three years and cost 36,940 American lives. In June 1950, thirty-five U.S. military advisers were sent to assist South Vietnam against communist insurgents.

1954 The U.S. funded and CIA and U.S. special forces orchestrated a coup that overthrew the government in Guatemala and installed Carlos Castillo Armas as president.

1955 American troops participated in a peacekeeping operation to establish a buffer zone between Costa Rica and Nicaragua. In Vietnam, American soldiers went into combat with South Vietnamese forces against the Vietcong and communists from North Vietnam.

1957 The CIA and special forces were successful in overthrowing Indonesia's government and installing one more friendly to the U.S.

1958 President Eisenhower sent 5,000 U.S. Marines to Beirut, Lebanon, when civil war in Iraq threatened to spill into Lebanon and Jordan.

1959 Troops were dispatched to Haiti to help put down a rebellion against Francois (Papa Doc) Duvalier.

1961 An invasion force of 1,500 Cuban nationals trained in the United States landed at the Bay of Pigs, Cuba, in an unsuccessful attempt to overthrow the communist government of Fidel Castro. The invasion was doomed when President John Kennedy withdrew U.S. air support at the last minute.

1962 Kennedy sent 5,000 troops, including a Marine battalion, to aid Thailand to assist in its resistance to threats from communist forces in Northern Laos. U.S. troops were part of a United Nations force that invaded the rogue African state of Katanga, which sparked a civil war when it attempted to secede from the Congo.

1964–1975 The U.S. commited to a major war in Vietnam. Claiming that North Vietnamese gunboats fired on U.S. warships in the Gulf of Tonkin, President Lyndon Johnson committed to sending an additional 200,000 troops to join the 16,000 "advisers" already in Vietnam. The conflict would claim 58,193 American lives.

1964 U.S. troops were dispatched to quell riots in Panama that ignited when American students displayed a United States flag. Twenty-nine Panamanians were killed and seventy injured in the fighting.

1965 In Zaire, Africa, the CIA staged a coup that put Mobutu Sese Seko in power. Fourteen thousand U.S. troops were sent to the Dominican Republic to assist that nation's military in opposing an attempt by communists to take over the island nation. In Laos, Green Berets were fighting a "secret war" against the Pathet Lao.

1966 Following a coup in Guatemala orchestrated by the CIA, U.S. troops openly assisted the new government in fighting communist guerrillas. A joint CIA and military operation in Bolivia captured guerrilla leader Che Guevara. Over objections by the U.S., he was promptly executed by the Bolivians.

1970 Under pressure from the Pentagon, President Nixon sent 18,000 troops to invade Cambodia. Under pressure from Congress, he pulled them out a few weeks later.

1971 The U.S. Air Force was called in to back a CIA-sponsored military coup in Bolivia that overthrew the leftist government of Juan Jose Torres.

1974 The U.S. Navy had to evacuate American citizens from the island of Cyprus when civil war broke out between Greek and Turkish Cypriots. A CIA attempt to start a coup ignited the hostilities.

1975 Marines, warships, and aircraft attacked Cambodia to rescue the crew of the captured U.S. merchantman *Mayaguez*. Fifteen Marines died in the action. Cambodia released the hostages. U.S. military advisers and arms were sent to Angola and Zaire, Africa, to counter takeover attempts by communist insurgents.

1979 With the Soviet invasion of Afghanistan, the U.S. supported rebel Afghan factions with arms and special forces advisers. Among the rebels was a Saudi national named Osama bin Laden.

1980 President Carter approved a rescue mission to liberate American hostages held in Iran. Ill-planned, the attempt failed when two helicopters collided at the staging area. Eight Marines were killed. Meanwhile, military advisers and arms poured into Nicaragua to assist the Contras attempting to overthrow the communist government.

1981 Fifty-five military advisers were sent to El Salvador to assist government forces in counterinsurgency training. In the Mediterranean, U.S. fighter planes from the carrier *Nimitz* were fired upon and responded by shooting down two Libyan jets.

1982 U.S. Marines were dispatched to Beirut, Lebanon, in an attempt to help stabilize the government. Eventually, 1,800 would be stationed there.

1983 A Hezbollah suicide bombing in Beirut claimed the lives of 241 Marines. The U.S. responded with air strikes on suspected Syrian terrorist positions. Two American planes were shot down and one pilot lost. Meanwhile, 2,000 U.S. Marines landed on the island nation of Grenada to rescue American students at a medical school and stop a communist takeover of the government. Killed in the fighting were twenty-nine Cuban and forty-nine Grenadian soldiers. Nineteen Americans died.

1985 To discourage the Sandinista government in Nicaragua from invading Honduras, the U.S. held a massive military exercise in Honduras that included warplanes, thirty-nine ships, and 7,000 troops.

1986 A Libyan patrol boat was sunk after firing on U.S. aircraft. Libyan leader Gadhafi called on Arabs worldwide to attack U.S. citizens. Libyan terrorists set off a bomb in a Berlin disco that killed two American soldiers and a Turkish woman and injured 230. President Reagan retaliated by sending F-111s to bomb Gadhafi's palace. In Bolivia, U.S. Army personnel and warplanes assisted in Operation Blast Furnace, which closed down twenty-one cocaine refineries. In Haiti, U.S. troops were landed to keep order following a coup that overthrew "Baby Doc" Duvalier.

1987 During the Iran–Iraq War, a U.S. fleet was sent to the Persian Gulf to protect shipments of oil from Kuwait.

1988 Missiles fired from the USS *Vincennes* by mistake brought down an Iranian passenger jet in the Persian Gulf, killing all 290 on board. Meanwhile, a U.S. force of 1,000 landed in Panama to protect American citizens and the Panama Canal.

1989 An additional 2,000 troops were sent to Panama and, following sporadic fighting, arrested President Manuel Noriega. Twenty-three U.S. soldiers were killed in the action. Noriega was brought to the U.S. where he was convicted of drug smuggling and imprisoned. In September, 100 U.S. military advisers were sent to Bolivia. Also, two U.S. fighter jets shot down two Libyan fighters over the Mediterranean.

1991 The invasion of Kuwait by Iraq triggered Operation Desert Shield / Desert Storm. Following heavy bombardment, the U.S. led a coalition of eighteen nations in an invasion of Iraq. The ground war lasted only three days. American deaths totaled 299, almost all of them from friendly fire or accidents. More than 100,000 Iraqis were killed.

1992 At the urging of the United Nations, President Bush sent U.S. troops to Somalia in response to a humanitarian crisis. Expected to last only a few months, Operation Restore Hope lasted two years and eventually involved 30,000 troops. In Iraq, U.S. fighter jets enforced no-fly zones to prevent Saddam Hussein's government from attacking Shiite and Kurdish civilians.

1993 Upon learning of a plot by Hussein to assassinate President Bush, U.S. naval forces unleash twenty-three cruise missiles against Iraq Intelligence Headquarters in Baghdad. Meanwhile, the U.S. Air Force participated with NATO to enforce a no-fly ban over Bosnia–Herzegovina, and President Clinton sent troops to Macedonia to contend with unrest on the Yugoslav border.

1994 The number of U.S. troops in Haiti reached 15,000 in the wake of a failed military coup. In Somalia a U.S. team sent to arrest a warlord is ambushed. In a brief but bitter street firefight, eighteen Americans and more than 300 Somalis are killed. Among those in Somalia urging attacks on Americans at the time was Osama bin Laden.

1996 The U.S. launched forty-four missiles into Iraq in retaliation for Iraqi forces invading Kurdish territory.

1998 In retaliation for al-Qaeda bombings of U.S. embassies in Africa, President Clinton authorizes launching of missiles at a chemical plant in Sudan and at terrorist training camps in Afghanistan. When weapons inspectors are ejected from Iraq, U.S. launches almost daily air strikes.

1999 With some 400 military advisers from the U.S. in Colombia to help fight drug cartels and insurgents, President Clinton expanded the program to include Peru, Ecuador, and Bolivia. In Europe, U.S. and NATO allies bombed Yugoslavia in an attempt to end attacks on Kosovo.

2001 September 11, 2001, marked the beginning of a U.S. War on Terror when Muslim terrorists crashed hijacked passenger jets into the World Trade Towers and the Pentagon, killing almost 3,000 citizens. In Operation

Enduring Freedom, U.S. forces joined with local war-lords to defeat the Taliban rulers in Afghanistan and pursue al-Qaeda terrorists into the mountains. To date 138 Americans have died in the conflict and more than 3,000 Afghans have been killed.

2002 U.S. military advisers were sent to the Philippines to assist the government in combating Muslim terrorists.

2003 On March 19, a massive bombardment of Baghdad signaled the beginning of Operation Iraqi Freedom and the invasion of Iraq by a coalition of armed forces led by the United States. By April 8, the Iraqi Army had been routed and the fighting was effectively over. The arrival of outside terrorists inspired a growing underground resistance designed to disrupt the formation of a new Iraqi government.

2004 An additional 12,000 troops were sent to Iraq, raising the U.S. force there to 150,000 to contend with suicide bombers and guerrilla fighters attempting to disrupt elections scheduled for January 2005. By the end of 2004, U.S. military deaths in Iraq had exceeded 1,300.

2005 Excluding those assigned to embassy security, as of January 2005, U.S. troops were stationed in the following countries: Canada, Cuba, Haiti, Honduras, Colombia, Belgium, Bosnia–Herzegovina, Germany, Greece, Iceland, Italy, Macedonia, Netherlands, Portugal, Serbia, Kosovo, Spain, Turkey, United Kingdom, Djibouti, Australia, Japan, South Korea, Philippines, Singapore, Thailand, Afghanistan, Bahrain, Diego Garcia, Egypt, Iraq, Qatar, and Saudi Arabia.

INDEX

ABOUT THE AUTHOR

Thomas Ayres was a veteran investigative reporter and an award-winning columnist. He wrote for the *Dallas Times Herald*, *Civil War Times*, *Columbiad*, and many other publications. His hometown was Jonesboro, Louisiana.